HELP IS ON THE WAY

Stay Up and Live Your Truth

HELP IS ON THE WAY

KOUNTRY WAYNE

with Mim Eichler Rivas

HARMONY

NEW YORK

harmonybooks.com

Harmony Books is a registered trademark, and the
Circle colophon is a trademark of Penguin Random House LLC.

Library of Congress Cataloging-in-Publication Data
Names: Kountry Wayne, 1987- author. | Rivas, Mim Eichler, author.
Title: Help is on the way : stay up and live your truth / Kountry Wayne with
Mim Eichler Rivas.
Description: New York : Harmony, 2023. | Includes index. |
Identifiers: LCCN 2022034930 (print) | LCCN 2022034931 (ebook) |
ISBN 9780593236475 (hardcover) | ISBN 9780593236499 (trade paperback) |
ISBN 9780593236482 (ebook)
Subjects: LCSH: Kountry Wayne, 1987– author. | Comedians—United
States—Biography. | Conduct of life. | LCGFT: Autobiographies.
Classification: LCC PN2287.K697 A3 2023 (print) |
LCC PN2287.K697 (ebook) | DDC 792.702/8092 [B]—dc23/eng/20220909
LC record available at https://lccn.loc.gov/2022034930
LC ebook record available at https://lccn.loc.gov/2022034931

ISBN 978-0-593-23647-5
Ebook ISBN 978-0-593-23648-2

Printed in the United States of America

Book design by Andrea Lau
Jacket design by Anna Bauer Carr
Jacket photographs by Amina Touray

10 9 8 7 6 5 4 3 2 1

First Edition

To the memory of Melissa Coney

Fear not, for I am with you;
be not dismayed, for I am your God;
I will strengthen you, I will help you,
I will uphold you with my righteous right hand.

ISAIAH 41:10

G rowing up in the Kountry as I did, stories well-told and lessons well-taught come from actual experience. That's what you'll find in this book, in recollections that are faithfully described—although certain names of people have been changed, along with identifying details associated with those individuals. Though I consider myself to be an excellent listener and I have pretty good recall, too, it's important to note that the words of dialogue I've included in actual conversations are not intended to be word-for-word reenactments. The exchanges I have written, however, are nonetheless recalled in the spirit of how they were spoken at the time.

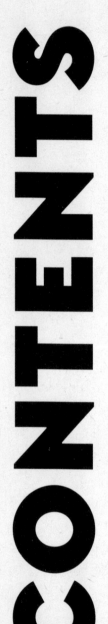

CONTENTS

PART II

PART III

The first time I met Kountry Wayne—not too many years ago—was at the Atlanta Comedy Theater where I had arrived to headline two sold-out shows that night. Wayne, in his late twenties and the father of nine kids, give or take, had just started to gain momentum as a stand-up, building on the success of his viral comedy videos that drew from his life growing up in a small "Kountry" town in southeast Georgia.

Now, I didn't know many of those details when he first approached me at the club after the second show was over. I'd come to Atlanta—always a welcoming city for me—as one of the first stops on a much longer tour. The small room at ACT gets packed to the gills, which makes it a great spot for testing out new material. You can gauge the response to a joke by how cold or hot it becomes in there, real fast.

Fortunately, the new stuff cranked the heat up right away and I had everybody in the club falling out laughing.

So, I was feeling pretty good as I stepped off the stage and spotted this young, eager-looking dude heading in my direction. The first thing I noticed was that he was wearing a Dallas Cowboys beanie hat—which takes some nerve in Atlanta, Georgia, where locals take pride in their Falcons. The best way to describe my first impression of Wayne Colley is that he seemed to shine with a bright light, was completely confident, self-assured, yet respectful and not afraid just to be a fan.

"Cedric," he began, and reached out to shake my hand, "that was amazing! You are one of my top favorite comedians ever." I thanked him as he went on to say, "Getting to see you in person is a highlight of my life!" He quickly added that he had been doing stand-up for a couple of years and was starting to spend more time out in LA, where he was booking some acting gigs, too. At that point he introduced himself.

"Kountry Wayne?" I said. "Cool." Intrigued, I asked, "What's your style of comedy?"

Not skipping a beat, he replied, "Classic entertainment mixed with stand-up." He said that was the blueprint he learned from comedy OGs like me.

I liked the fact that he made no effort to talk any other way than how he did—with a thick Kountry drawl. It's not the white *Suthe'n kinda drawwwwl* that sounds like too much sugar in your sweet tea. Black Kountry dialect is almost slangy, with dropped consonants at the end of words, and fresh expressions you may never have heard that can be cutting without you even knowing it.

I said something along the lines of "Keep on doing what you're doing and I have the feeling we'll all be seeing a lot of you in the comedy world."

"Yeah, *fo sho*," he said, or words to that effect, thanked me, and took off.

After meeting Wayne that first time I started to follow him on social media and was impressed. Over the next couple of years, his star continued to rise and his orbit expanded—from dating superstars to doing film and TV appearances, to becoming an entrepreneur, producer, and philanthropist. By 2019, Kountry Wayne was defying all the odds and, in my view, had emerged as the leader of the new school of comedians who understood how to build an audience in the twenty-first century—both in the viral universe and in brick-and-mortar comedy venues of all sizes. For that reason, I wanted to lean toward his experience and open whatever doors I could for him. In the process, I reached out to him to talk about potentially developing some content together—and what followed has been and continues to be immensely rewarding for the both of us.

As I explained to Wayne, at the time when I was just getting a foothold in comedy, there weren't many mentors who were able to take young comics of our generation under their wings. Nobody had been there to make a way for Richard Pryor and the same was true for Eddie Murphy. Fortunately for Eddie, he had been given a massive launch from *SNL* and between stand-up and an epic string of blockbuster hit movies he soon blazed a trail of his own. When Chris Rock got his own boost from *SNL*, that's where things changed somewhat and Eddie Murphy stepped in to help Chris gain a credibility as a stand-up in a much faster amount of time than it would have taken on his own. When I was getting started, I had the great fortune to connect with

Steve Harvey—and after we worked together on *Kings of Comedy*, the two of us would take turns pulling the other in on whatever latest project we were on.

Wayne ate up this history as if it were biblical. He could sit and ask questions for hours about how to achieve the same success (or greater) as his early influences. He has that visionary (hustler) mentality and is always looking for how to top others as well as himself. Wayne is serious about making all the right moves and he is someone who doesn't let much grass grow under his feet. He might ask, "Ced, what were the lessons you had to learn to really make it?"

The two main lessons I shared with him were ones he had learned already—and are included up ahead in *Help Is on the Way*—but they may have been lessons he needed to be reminded of. First, as I tell everyone trying to make it in entertainment or in any competitive field, *you can't skip steps*. The Kountry Wayne version of this is, "Mind Your Business." It's true. You not only have to build each step of your ladder before you can ascend it, but if you rush and don't take pride in your creation, no amount of success is going to make you feel like you've made it. Plus, if you skip one of those rungs, you won't have anywhere to land if you do have to take a step down. Something Wayne learned on his own, that I believe in strongly, is that you have to build your career with love, as something you nourish. You birth it, you raise it, you treat it like a baby or a beloved pet that you care for unconditionally and that will care for you back.

Unlike many of the Internet comics who manage to build massive audiences without stepping onto a stage, Wayne has done both—cultivating his family of fans who have been with him on his ride in his social media comedy sketch series *and* in the clubs and theaters where he is headlining and selling out more and more. Wayne has put in the work, and that integrity is why so many OG Comics respect him and the route he has taken to get where he is.

The second lesson I shared with Wayne was one I had to learn the hard way, and it was something he knew well—*Live your truth*. Early in my career, I didn't have the wisdom to know that if you try to change yourself to conform to what you think the powers-that-be want from you, it can do you in. The lesson came after I had more or less booked a TV show after having the door opened for me by Steve Harvey. The deal was all but sealed. So I was flown to New York to do a showcase for the network—just to make everybody laugh and feel good about casting me, I guess. Steve was there to be a part of what was going to be the next exciting chapter in both of our comedy lives. Every white executive at the network had gathered in a room with a catered gourmet meal and I started to think twice about my risqué material and my St. Louis, Missouri, raucous delivery, and I decided to change my dialect and make it more everyman midwestern or something and even my delivery point. On the fly, I just decided to change my whole set. Nobody laughed. Nobody cracked a smile. The more I tried, the icier it got in that room. This wasn't bombing in front of just any crowd. These were the network executives who had hired me already, based on Steve Harvey's belief in me.

Inside I was dying because a lot of the executives didn't know who I was and my bombing so bad was going to make them question Steve's judgment, too. Before I could wrap up my set, out of the corner of my eye, I watched Steve come up on stage, grab the mic from me and cuss all of those exec's asses out! It was the opposite of what I was trying to do. He was so authentically himself, it was hilarious to hear him cuss at them for not laughing at me. "Look at y'all. You got somewhere to go?" There was a beat before he went further, asking, "What happened?

Y'all ran out of crudities and ranch? Are you hungry or something?" Steve Harvey got every single one of them to laugh at themselves, to the point of tears running down their faces because he was that funny.

Later, Steve emphasized the lesson, telling me, "You should never change your set for somebody else. Be who you are authentically, that's what makes you different, that's your edge." He admitted that it might not work in every setting but that's the risk you take and if you bomb being yourself, that's not on you, and so be it.

That has always been one of the most important lessons in my life and as you're going to read shortly, it has always been a pivotal lesson for Kountry Wayne, the one and only. The father of now ten kids, Wayne has come a long way since we first met. In the summer of 2022, I caught his act for the first time when his Straight Out the Mud tour brought him to LA as part of the Netflix Is a Joke festival. I expected him to bring down the house and I was not disappointed in the least. He exceeded expectations and I was so proud to see him up there—working clean, by the way—and as commanding and professional as much older show business veterans. His show was part seduction and part revival.

And that's kind of how I feel about Wayne's book. You are in for a rags-to-riches story full of inspiration and practical guidance. He really believes in passing on the goods that he has learned to you.

Whatever our conversations, business or personal, I always feel with Kountry Wayne that he *chooses* to live in the light—which is the real secret of how he stays up. And he is teaching the rest of us how to do the same.

Cedric the Entertainer

WELCOME!

Growing up in Millen, Georgia—population about 3,500 (feels like 350)—I never needed to introduce myself to anyone. In pit-stop Kountry towns like Millen, most everybody knows everybody. Folks are just naturally *nosy*. Not to mention *bored*. They get to know your name, the names of your momma, your daddy, your kids, the whole rest of the family, the address where you stay, where you work, what cars y'all drive, and every other kind of whatnot.

Now, in the City—in Atlanta, for example, where I spent every summer up until the tenth grade—you learn to introduce yourself right up front. *Fast*. Otherwise, City folk will judge you in a heartbeat. If you don't introduce yourself first, somebody will decide to give you a name and—*bam*—it's stuck on you for good.

That's what happened to me in my teens when I started to talk about making it in show business one day. My Atlanta relatives and friends would scoff. They'd say, "*You?* You too Kountry to make it." That's code for *slow*. And that's more or less how I got my nickname in my early teens—*Kountry Wayne*. The funny part was that in Millen nobody called me that for years. In the small-town way of thinking, sadly, anybody who had serious ambition was just being biggidy. Like uppity. In fact, they called me City slick. I was even accused of being *too* City. That's code for *fast*.

Was I too slow or too fast?

Neither, if you ask me. So I learned not to care what anyone else had to say. Instead, I took the best parts of being both. At an early age, I became the Man in the Town. Millen was like my own mini New York City. Once I left my hometown for good and started to get better-known in more populated places like Statesboro, Savannah, and Atlanta, I brought the best of the real Kountry with me.

One way I did that, first in throwing parties and eventually as a host in my own club, was by introducing myself and going all out to invite people to "*get on down,*" as we say in Millen. "*Get on down!*" is how we make you feel at home and encourage you to set your worries aside. At least for the time being. "*Get on down!*" is the same as saying, "*C'mon on in, pull up a chair, take a load off, visit, maybe get something to eat, listen to stories, laugh, be entertained, and possibly find new strength to take on tomorrow.*"

So *get on down* and get comfortable. In other words, "*Welcome!*"

You can call me Kountry Wayne or Dewayne Colley or KW or just Wayne. Some of y'all might know me from my viral skits on social media where I've made millions of dollars and gained millions of followers and fans in a way that almost nobody can figure out. (Hint: It's called an algorithm and I learned it from studying Albert Einstein, an

OG hustler if ever there was one, and I'm happy to share his secrets with you.) Some of y'all probably have heard rumors that I have tens of thousands of children—as many kids as David in the Bible had sheep in his flock.

Naw, that's crazy!

Full disclosure: I've got ten kids (at this count). I know you might be wondering, *Kountry Wayne, you're only thirty-four. With all them kids and five baby mamas, what's up?* The short answer is there was *nuthin* else to do in Millen for fun. The longer answer is I love women. Every kind of woman.

That's just a fact. Of course, I've also worn a lot of other hats besides being a playa and a ladies' man. I'm a (former) hustler, it's true, but today, in addition to being a stand-up comic, I'm a legit entrepreneur with successful businesses and a mess of folks on payroll. I've also been drug- and alcohol-free all my life, I'm a vegan, and I'm an evangelical water drinker. Water is the greatest untold secret to the good life. If you aren't drinking water right at this minute, go get yourself a pitcher and a glass and start living better now. Also, I'm a rapper, a dancer, an athlete, a model, an actor, a writer/director/producer, a teacher, and a preacher, not to mention a love-and-prosperity-advice guru who reps Jesus—and who gives praise every day to God and respect to all people of faith, regardless of your beliefs and religion.

Who knows? I might add a few more titles to my résumé in the future. Mayor, Oscar winner, real estate developer, and, on the personal side of things, maybe even husband. The story is not yet written.

For now, making people laugh is my main hustle. Y'all might know that I work clean in comedy. My motto is *"I can make your stomach bust and I ain't got to cuss."* Watch out, 'cause I pop waist trainers!

Not all the content here is PG, though. So, be forewarned. Now and then I might get kinda drippy. When that happens, you know what time it is. It's time for the sauce that's got a kick to it—not too freaky but enough spice to be real. In those instances, you might hear from some of my alter egos—characters from my skits, like Drip and Buddy, who will chime in with their own outspoken grown-folk advice.

If you're not familiar with him, Drip is a dope dealer trying to go legit as a rapper but he's still in the streets. Even so, he lives by a code: no guns, no violence. Despite his Cartier diamond eyeglasses and fourteen-karat gold teeth, Drip avoids flashing too much paper around. On the other hand, there's Buddy, a white-haired sugar daddy who has a large roll of hundreds in his pocket and a long list of phone numbers for the lovely *ladeeees* he protects from real sex predators.

Drip and Buddy are based on aspects of myself and on some of the real-life characters I watched growing up. You might say they are who I would have ended up becoming *if* I hadn't learned the lessons I'm about to share with you all. If I had stopped pushing myself to grow, I could have settled for life as Drip. Sometimes I see him in my rearview mirror and that keeps me motivated to continue to evolve. Most of us know a Buddy or two—the men who pretend to be there for women but are really only out for themselves. That's a dead-end future in every situation. At the same time, there's a side to Buddy that's refreshing because, like Drip, he knows who he is and who he isn't.

Buddy and Drip represent where a lot of us are at different points in our lives. Their examples show us how common it is to be in a place where we shine bright for a moment but soon burn out. Instead, we can choose a more rewarding future by setting foot onto the paths where we can sustain our light.

Whether or not you have watched my videos or just have heard of me—or you were told by a friend that you had to read this book!—it does *not* matter. What matters is that you, reader/listener, are here, a guest of honor, and that you get the blessings through the lessons I've learned from all that I've worked so hard to attain. They've given me practical guidance that I continue to apply to this day—as I work even harder to continue growing and making sure those blessings keep on coming.

One of the questions I hear everywhere I go is *"Kountry Wayne, where do you get your drive? What motivates you to go so hard all the time?"*

My answer is simple: child support.

That's a joke, but it's true. Child support has a way of making you grind like you could be broke in a week if you didn't. That may be an exaggeration, but I'm here to say that hell hath no fury like a baby mama when her man is late on child support. Trust me on this. If you ever can't find me performing or making videos or out selling books, I'll probably be hiding somewhere in Georgia to avoid baby mamas swinging baseball bats at my head. It's a law of the universe: *The more success you have, the more your monthly child support goes up.*

The truth is that my ten kids are my greatest blessings by far and my most important sources of motivation. That's really the answer to the question I hear most often: *"How, after everything, did you get out the mud?"*

From the beginning, I've had faith. It's the same faith my great grandmomma—and maybe yours—used to have sitting up on her porch, rocking in her chair, drinkin' lemonade, and sayin', "Everything gonna be alright." It's the same faith that convinced me in tough times—help is on the way and if I do my part to put in the work, there is more ahead than a small-town life.

There was a time when everything I thought could destroy me was there to teach me how to do my part before help arrived. These same experiences later turned out to give me superpowers. The lessons I learned took me out of one of the roughest places in America to a richer, fuller, wiser, and more abundant life. And that is what I want for you. Whatever your situation, I've got fourteen *poppin' principles* (and then some), which can be applied immediately to make a difference in your life. These lessons come from my life experiences, and from the experiences of members of my family and community. Some of the principles come from observing the paths pursued by successful individuals I've met or read about. After all, they say a smart man learns from his mistakes but a wise man learns from the mistakes of others. I also say that other people's lessons can be your blessings, too.

If that sounds like a hustle, why not check out what's on the menu first? You may have a great life that could be better or you may have trouble finding hope. The principles I'm here to share are relevant in the best times and the darkest times. They are a proven product. Test them yourself, apply them to your life. Let them be a solution to your problems, a kick-starter to realizing your dreams, and a magnet to bring you the peace, love, and riches that are exactly what's intended for you.

You might not need much more than to laugh or cry or feel a boost in your spirit. Maybe you are fed up and want to hear me vent. I got that for you. Maybe you are done being in the street life but can't figure out how to find the exit. Don't worry, I got you. Maybe you had your heart broke, or maybe you just *are* broke. Whatever. Know that you are covered here. Help is on the way. And here in these chapters we create our own luck and our own opportunities. And our own story. Because we *can*.

Bottom line, this is my story and I made a promise to myself to tell it the way it happened. It's not all squeaky-clean or told in a way just to make you laugh, but really to make you think. Both, I hope! We all have the power to choose to make life better—not just for ourselves but for the world. Even in troubled times. You have limitless riches that you don't even know about, but that will be revealed once you learn not to care what anyone else thinks, or how they judge you.

You are getting all that in one book. So *get on down,* the way we do in Millen, Georgia. We got Jesus poppin', we got the angels poppin', and we got your Higher Power and the Universe poppin' with love for you.

Let *that* sizzle in your spirit.

PART I

CHAPTER 1

AW, HELL

Sometimes All You Have Is Your Pride

There is no better hustle than doing what you love so much you'd do it for free—and then still getting paid for it. On top of that, as a working comedian, I feel truly blessed to be given the gift of making people laugh so they feel better for a little while or longer. The way I see it, what I do is a healing, spiritual profession. They don't call it "divine comedy" for *nuthin.*

I'm even more proud of what I do for a living because a) I didn't fit the mold of what Hollywood and the show business system considered acceptable and b) I refused to give up after multiple doors were shut in my face. But most of all, I'm proud that c) instead of waiting for opportunities, I decided to create my own content and my own company and it proved to be more lucrative than I ever dreamt—for me and a bunch of other folks. Going against the grain, I have shown that you can be Kountry simple to break into the big time. That's what I did—using only a cell phone, original story ideas, and God's greatest creation: human beings.

No one took me seriously at first, but thanks to my pride, I didn't listen. Even some of my trusted advisors worried that the Internet skits were just cute but not worth investing in, only to find out later that those early videos were the key to every success that followed. Those simple skits were like David's rock and Hollywood was like Goliath. You know how that one ends.

Most people—maybe everyone—expected me to fail. At times I was discouraged, but giving up and admitting to failure was not gonna happen. Why not? Plain and simple, I was too proud to throw in the towel and have others be proven right.

If you look at all the billion-dollar businesses that made it out of someone's garage, you might hear stories about hard work, innovation, and good business instincts. Not many of those billionaires will admit to the power of pride. Of course, I know pride is one of the seven deadly sins and it can get you in trouble and make you too vain or un-realistic about what you can or can't do. But, as this first lesson tells us, *sometimes all you have is your pride.*

Pride, after all, can direct you to your true assets. It took me a long time to appreciate how much wisdom and humor was all around me—right there in Millen, Georgia. Of course, I never bought into the stereotype of Kountry people being "slow" and I felt that somebody like me could change that narrative. That's why I related to the legend-ary rapper André 3000 of the Atlanta-based duo Outkast when he spoke up at the 1995 Source Awards by saying, "The South got some-thing to say!"

The challenge for any of us from the Kountry—whether you're Black/white/brown, or anything in between—is that other people like to call us ignorant. The thing is, *ignorant* only means lacking information. And that's true no matter where you go. So you have to make a choice, every day, to challenge your own ignorance and to build up your appreciation for all you've got to learn.

The part that makes me proud about being Kountry is that without the City distractions, you can become a deep thinker. You don't need as much stuff. In the Kountry, everything becomes a lot more *simple*. It's down-to-earth wisdom. If you want to understand the most complicated issues in the universe, just like solving problems in math or science, you break it all down to its simplest form, and slow way down. Back to basics. I'm proud of that.

Once upon a time, we were all Kountry—back in the olden days when there was nothing but land and farms, before big buildings and social media. Back then, all you needed was a horse to get a girl. Or, yeah, let's say a *big* horse.

Nowadays, you have to get a thousand-horsepower engine with a name like Ferrari to get that girl. Not as simple.

Most people all over the United States have some kind of roots in the South and some Kountry in their blood. You know how you can tell if it's in someone's DNA? By how easy it is to make them laugh. Good storytellers and good story listeners come from out in the sticks, where there's no entertainment and you have to pass the time somehow. If you can't find a way to be funny in the Kountry or if you don't know somebody who's funny, then you are missing out.

When you take pride in your roots, wherever they are, you can turn the world that shaped you into your brand—and make fun of it and make fun of yourself in the process. Pride can be powerful and lucrative. At the very least, it can help you keep your head up when you most need to. The key is learning how to use the pride you have.

So let's get into the action—starting with an event that took place in March 2008. This was long before I even dreamt of being a comedian.

Pride versus Vanity

There is a huge difference between having pride and thinking you can talk your way out of accepting the consequences of your own actions. That difference was very much in my head as I approached the main entrance to the old Jenkins County Courthouse in downtown Millen.

Naw, wait, that's an exaggeration. To be honest, Millen has no *down*town. There's a hint of a town center—a few small businesses, a police station with all of four jail cells, and maybe two other modest municipal office buildings. And then, plunked in the middle of all that, lost in time, is the courthouse. Dating back to 1910, the courthouse was built at a point in history when Millen was seen as a place of importance—after being named the county seat for the recently formed Jenkins County.

I'm not sure why they chose Millen for county seat. It has never been a destination on its own, rather a train junction for two different railways. More or less, it is a whistle-stop from the time when cotton was king. In fact, in 1852 Millen got its name in honor of the superintendent of the railroad of Southeast Georgia. Whenever people ask where Millen is in relation to other cities—like Atlanta to the northwest (about 176 miles) or Savannah to the southeast (about 85 miles)—

most Kountry folk will point in the direction of where it is and say, "Over yonder, a ways." If a town is closer, like Statesboro, 30 miles or so to the south, the answer is just, "Over yonder."

With directions like that, you could easily get lost, but not if you're looking for the courthouse. It is easily the largest, nicest building in Millen. In March of 2008, as I approached the entrance, I maybe would have liked it more if I wasn't about to have a sentencing hearing *and* if it wasn't designed in that Southern plantation style that white people still love to build in Georgia.

For $5,000, I had hired a lawyer who advised me to take a plea deal—guilty of possession of cocaine with intent to sell. This could mean a mandatory sentence of six to eight months in prison. Or longer. Still, with a couple prior offenses, though minor, a jury trial could get me up to ten years in jail. That was the reality of being even a small-time hustler. So was the fact that when you're Black and poor in a backward Kountry town like Millen, you have few legit avenues for income outside of picking peanuts.

My lawyer, Jerry Daniels, did manage to convince the DA to make it an *open-ended* plea deal—meaning a judge would hear me as to why I should be given ten years' probation instead of getting locked up for 180 to 240 days (or more). My lawyer had reassured me that, all things considered, "Welllllllll, it could be a lot worse."

Then we found out that I was being seen by Judge Turner, the meanest, maddest, throw-the-book-at-you-just-because-he-could kind of judge.

Inside my brain, as I made my way up the sidewalk to the courthouse, I kept thinking, *Wayne you done messed up now and you've only got yourself to blame.* But then again, you'd think all the police waiting by the entrance to the courthouse would have had some other small-town crimes to solve instead of standing around foaming at the mouth waiting for me to get my jail sentence.

That's when doubts started to set in. I reminded myself that, when it came to being likable and using my words to get myself out of tough spots, I didn't have a half-bad track record. But then I thought of that line of Scripture—you know the one: "Pride goeth before a fall." And I went back to worrying.

As a child, I always would hear Bible warnings that preachers and teachers used to try to impress upon me. It didn't matter if we were at any one of the three places where I used to go to church with family members—the Bethel AME my momma liked to attend, the Baptist church my daddy's momma preferred, or the Kingdom Hall of Jehovah's Witnesses that my momma's momma frequented. I enjoyed being at all the different houses of worship. Mainly, I loved hearing any conversation about God. Whenever the preachers talked about pride, they seemed to whip their heads around and stare right at me, like I really needed to know about words engraved on clay tablets in the Book of Proverbs, however many thousands of years before my birth in December 1987. But I'd sit there as a little kid and think, *Am I prideful?* Then I'd answer, *Maybe, except what else do I have* but *my pride?* Swag and confidence were given to me by both my parents, especially my momma. If pride was a problem, I couldn't do much about it. My attitude was, *I mean, what if I am proud?* Besides, what's a little fall now and then? Eventually, I read the real passage from Scripture and learned that the words translated more closely to, "Pride goes before destruction, a haughty spirit before a fall."

Was I a haughty hustler? Not as far as I was concerned. In fact, up until this time, I wasn't big in the streets at all. My operation in those days was more or less a small traphouse in another town about twenty minutes from Millen. I never did business with any kind of violent or crazy individuals and wanted *nuthin* to do with anybody who had guns. The rule was that I only sold recreational quantities and would cut anyone off who was acting like they'd had too much. Knowing what substance abuse had done, one way or another, to almost everyone in my family, I never got high in my whole life, which kept me from the common pitfall of dipping into my own supply.

But maybe, I thought, as I looked straight ahead at the courthouse, *I might have become OVERLY prideful.* What other explanation was there for how I'd ended up in this predicament with the law in the first place?

Everybody's Got a Hustle

Well, the events that led to my run-in with the law did involve pride, I admit. But there's another common answer to the question of why people choose to deal drugs in the first place—limited options. For most of my life growing up, even minimum wage jobs were scarce. There was no Walmart in Millen. There was no McDonald's until only recently. By the time I got to high school, there were only three manufacturing plants left in town—Jockey, of underwear fame; Metal Industries, a window manufacturer; and Bellcrest, a mobile home maker. Those were good, skilled jobs with benefits, but openings were rare. Then, with the beginning of the recession of 2007–8, the plants shut down and all the factory jobs went overseas. That fully destroyed our economy. For anyone Black in Millen, after that, finding a legit job was like winning the lottery.

You could live off the land, of course. We weren't that far from the days of slavery and sharecropping. Lots of Black folks I knew were still waiting for their forty acres and a mule. When I was little, in fact, one of my grandmommas was still picking cotton. Or you could pick peanuts at harvest time or slaughter hogs. That was *not* gonna be my future!

As jobs vanished over the years, one after the other, my daddy and uncles and other family members became hustlers. It was a way of life. In Millen, only Black folk who owned legit businesses were perceived as truly successful. Otherwise, the way things were, you either became a drug dealer or you were *nuthin.*

Being a hustler of any kind in the Kountry is not the same as hustling in the City—where the competition over turf and customers is intense. City police are hard-core and only pretend not be racist, even when they are profiling you. Kountry police are straight-to-the-point racist and they will just call you the N-word like it's a compliment.

The police in Millen are known far and wide for giving out tons of speeding tickets. Talk about police pride. What makes the police hustle so successful is Millen's sweet geographical location at the intersection of US Route 25 and State Route 17.

That might sound like *nuthin* to you, but our spot on the map has become famous for being an excellent speed trap. Millen itself is only 3.6 square miles, out in the middle of nowhere. So, if you sneeze while driving through, you miss the town almost completely. But if you happen to be going faster than the speed limit . . . *BAM!* You'll be caught by radar and surrounded by prideful Millen traffic police officers looking to write more than their quota of speeding tickets.

Other than speeding tickets, though, our police don't get to make a lot of important busts. There's a regular sort of cat-and-mouse game that goes on between law enforcement and dope dealers. Everybody knows who's who and what's what. Everybody also knows that when the economy's in trouble, already poor people get even poorer and get desperate, and do what they have to do to survive.

One of the reasons I tried to keep my business outside Millen was that local law enforcement knew the yellow and red Crown Victoria with the twenty-two-inch chrome rims was mine. They pulled me over so often, but could never find anything on me, so I used to jokingly say, "Aw, you can't never catch me, I'm just too smart for y'all." Somehow, I managed to outwit them, and they couldn't seem to get anything on me.

In the fall of 2007, that prideful brag had finally gotten on the last nerve of one Officer Brad Adams, my archnemesis. Officer Adams had started taking an extra interest in keeping tabs on me and routinely looked for any reason to pull me over.

On the night that would have been his big drug bust, I had over an ounce on me—that's a felony possession with a trafficking charge, enough to send me right to the penitentiary for ten years. Not knowing who had pulled me over and told me to get out of my car, when I stepped out of my car and saw Officer Adams standing there, smirking, my stomach twisted up.

Brad Adams was twenty-five at most, about five or six years older than me, bald and skinny, and really a Kountry boy. In his street clothes, he was not that intimidating. But in his uniform, on the job, he obviously had been studying TV cops and he tried to act how a big-city detective would. He carried himself like a coiled snake, ready to spring on you if he could find any shred of a cause to do so. It was funny because Brad Adams wasn't that snake guy really. Not to mention, he was in Millen. But he had developed an unhealthy obsession with me.

Thankfully, earlier that evening I had thought to put my drug stash on the inside of the gas tank, where you'd normally put the hose in to fill it up. As hard as he searched my car and me, the one place Officer

Adams didn't look was in the gas tank. He almost did but when he went to push the gas tank button, miraculously he hit the trunk button right next to it instead. I thought he hit the gas tank—which made me almost faint—but as the trunk flew up, I knew I was alright.

"You're free to go Dewayne. I'll get you next time," he grumbled.

It's possible . . . Yeah, I confess, I might have jokingly said, "Brad, I told you, you just can't catch me. I'm always a step ahead," or something prideful and foolish like that as I got back in my way-too-flashy car and drove off.

About two weeks later, September 23, 2007, to be precise, around ten o'clock at night, I'd just pulled out of the driveway of a friend's place—where illegal activities were suspected—when I realized that I was being followed. Bad news. *The good news,* I thought proudly, *was that I was smart enough to be driving my sister's 2000 Dodge Ram—not my Ronald McDonald–looking 1995 Crown Victoria.* So, whoever was following me most likely didn't know it was me in the car. Even so, whoever it was proceeded to signal for me to pull over.

When the officer got out of the car, I could see it was Matthew, a pretty cool Kountry boy who, in my high school days, once let me go after catching me in a churchyard going at it with a girl. Matthew was a farmer when he wasn't being a police. Relieved that it wasn't Brad, I wasn't nervous at all when he told me to exit the car. Before I did so, I thought fast and did the first thing that came to mind, putting my stash, only a half-ounce or under, down my pants.

"Matthew," I said, getting out of the car, friendly but also insulted, "why'd you pull me over, man? I ain't do *nuthin.*"

"Oh, hey, Dewayne," he said, kind of disappointed—like it would be a waste of time 'cause nobody ever got me on anything in Millen.

Matthew snooped around the car and then started to do a half-hearted search of me. Keeping cool, I braced myself just as he was about to pat me down in my grown-man area, where I'd put my stash. All of a sudden, Matthew stopped, saying, "Hold on a minute. Don't move." Walking fast, he went back to his patrol car and picked up the phone to call for backup.

The voice on his car speaker sounded like Brad Adams. "Who you say you got?"

Matthew repeated, louder, "I got one of the Colley brothers."

"Which one?"

"Dewayne."

"I'm on the way!" The excitement in Brad's voice was clearly audible.

Oh, Lord. Matthew had patted me down somewhat but I knew Brad Adams was going to search me for real.

By then I was not feeling good about things and as Matthew started walking back to me, making small talk, I caught a glimpse of another patrol car pulling up. Sure enough, the officer stepped out and it was definitely Brad.

"Man," I said to the both of them, and then paused, coming up with a strategy. All I had to do was talk my way out of having Brad Adams catch me with my stash. I said, "Matthew just patted me down. See y'all doing me wrong, and I didn't do . . ."

BOOM! Mid-sentence, I turned and did what any Millen high school athlete and basketball player would have done. *I ran!* Like the wind. Fast and furious.

As soon as I bolted, Brad pulled out his taser gun and fired it—and only missed because I had run so fast I was already out of range by the time he shot at me. The two officers gave chase but I lost them in the night dust and didn't stop running until I spotted a house, next to fields of some sort, where I could hide. Thinking they'd never look for a little package of contraband out here, I threw my stash in a bush as fast as I could. In hindsight, that was my mistake, I threw it out too early.

For the next hour, I lay low. Additional back-up patrol cars showed up nearby. The new police searched out in the fields using their flashlights but didn't come close to where I was. Eventually, they gave up.

Finally, relieved that the coast was clear, and tired, too, I got up. The reality, and I knew it as I silently headed back home on foot, was that I was probably going to have to turn myself in the next day. Right then, in the dark, I brushed past something—or somebody—all in black who had a police badge on his shirt. I had passed that person's shoulder and paused to say, "Man, it look like you all out here looking for someone tonight, ain't ya?"

The voice that came back at me belonged to Brad Adams. "Yeah," he answered, "and if he takes one more step, I'm gonna blow his head off!"

Then Brad told me to get down on the ground. Next thing I knew, he had called Sheriff Tim Fields, a tall, stern fellow who reminded me of a poor man's Tom Hanks. Think of Forrest Gump when he was in the military. Sheriff Fields showed up, his arms folded with satisfaction, as he gloated right along with Brad. The sheriff had it in for me almost as much as Brad because he was convinced that I was messing with his daughter. His *white* daughter. Not true. Least not at that time.

Sheriff Fields said to Brad, "Y'all can shut down the search." He must have figured that I'd gotten rid of whatever it was that I had no doubt had on me and, in all likelihood, it was not about to be found.

Brad refused, saying, "Sheriff, I wanna wait to get the dogs out here." Drug-sniffing dogs.

Sheriff Fields again said, "That's a waste, Brad. *Nuthin* has turned up by now, you know he got rid of it. Best shut it down."

Brad insisted that since the dogs were already on their way, there was no point in stopping the search. He would not give up. His own life depended on finding the stash and he could almost taste his glory of being the one to say, "I got Dewayne Colley." He was that close. He was over the damn moon, as he put me in handcuffs and walked me to his patrol car, all while calling in the news that he was bringing me to the station. "We got you," he said, congratulating himself. "We finally got you."

"Oh, hush, Brad had me the other night with a whole ounce in the gas tank, but you were too stupid to look for it. And you didn't get me, Matthew got me." If they did find the bag I'd tossed under some bushes, all they would have on me was possession with intent—a much lighter charge that could be probation or a shorter sentence to be served in a detention facility.

Was my comment too prideful or me just running my mouth?

A week later, my brother would answer that question after being pulled over. He would call me to say, "Dewayne you gotta stop cussing out the police." Guess where the first place was that the police looked for his stash? You are right—his gas tank! Luckily, they found *nuthin* because he had wedged his contraband, some crack cocaine, between his butt cheeks.

I may have responded with a very Drip line: "Yuh, yuh, good job, bro. You got your crack in your crack! Nobody ever wanna go lookin' there!"

We busted a gut laughing.

We had to laugh. Things were not flowing in my favor.

At that same point in the night of September 23, when Brad Adams had refused to give up the search for whatever he was sure I'd stashed somewhere out in the field, the sheriff had made arrangements for me to be taken to the station and booked for the night. When I arrived, I recognized my baby mama's brother, who had coincidentally been brought in earlier. Somehow, he had access to somebody's cell phone and was able to call his sister and let her know I was in jail.

From a nearby police scanner, a dispatch made it clear that Brad and the dogs were still trying to find the drugs I'd ditched.

A feeling of surrender or exhaustion came over me. Was this the life I really wanted? I had two young children already and I had a prideful thought: *Am I not worthy of something more than being a hustler?* This must have been where I first began to suspect that pride can work for you or against you. Taunting the police is where pride can hurt you. But if your pride whispers in your ear that you could actually be great without the streets, that's a moment to prize. That, right there, is help on the way, trying to reach you.

The truth is, I'd known for a while that this way of life wasn't leading anywhere good. Without many other options that would give me enough to support my growing family, I didn't know exactly how to get out of the game. All I knew was I just wanted to win. I wanted to win so much that I would rather die before I would give in and lose.

Less than three months away from my twentieth birthday, as I sat in the jail cell, I'd already concluded that too many Black, poor Kountry people get to where they're afraid to be great. In places like Millen, you are not encouraged to have pride or ambition or to even dream of greatness. For Black folks, I think it goes back to slavery, when we got whipped for having any kind of ideas about moving up in the world. Somehow, all these years later, too many of us are in the habit of whipping ourselves before the system can. It's like we'd rather beat ourselves down than be a threat to the people who have power over us. Trust me, you gotta have some skills to whip yourself on top of how badly the system really is rigged. That's because in a Kountry town, it's still plantation rules.

When the voice of pride says, "Be great!" and the voice of fear says, "Don't shine too bright," the contrast tells you what you need to do.

My pride pushed me to recognize that having a legit job sounded like paradise compared to being locked up in a holding cell at the Podunk police station in Millen. Not to mention that there had been a few warning signs before this night. If God was trying to tell me something, I'd better listen.

The way I saw my situation was, if they *did not* find the drugs, I had my Get Out of Jail Free card. If they *did* find them, that was a sign I needed to quit. The last time I'd gone to jail was just for running from the police in Statesboro and they kept me there for seven miserable days while they searched, but never found what I'd ditched. So, in my logic, as long as they couldn't find anything with an intent to sell it, why get out of the game? All I had was my pride.

With that, I fell into a deep sleep, and when I woke up, I heard my baby mama's brother saying my name. "Wayne, Wayne!"

I sat up. "Why you wakin' me?"

"They found something," he said. The story he had heard from the police was that the dog couldn't find anything and everybody was about to leave when the dog had to pee. Wouldn't you know it? The dog went over right where I'd ditched that package of cocaine and peed on it. The dog turned around to sniff at where he had just peed and Brad and the other police came running over.

All I could say was, "I'll be doggone."

By the time they released me, I'd been in the Millen jailhouse for three days. Reality was setting in. I went to stay at my baby mama's house to spend time with my two young sons. My children always have had a way of helping me see the bigger picture. Maybe you have someone (or a few someones) in your life who reminds you of what matters most and helps you see your way forward. If you are ever struggling to find your pride, hopefully there are loved ones who look at you like you are the hero of their life. You ask yourself, how can I be worthy of that? You'll get answers right away.

Even though I had decided this was *it,* that I was ready to leave hustling for good, in the scheme of things I did know that getting out once and for all was *not* gonna be so easy. But I definitely was done for the time being—given two previous misdemeanor convictions and a possible felony charge looming up ahead. Earlier in the year, I had quit dealing after a couple of close calls. Since then, I had been working a legit job at Metal Industries, handling sheets of glass for windows, and had only recently gone back to having a side hustle to try to cover the costs of a growing family. After my arrest, though, I became a born-again working man, and was keeping on the right side of the law. Everything was back to bringing home the weekly paycheck and lying low and slow. Then, a couple days into January 2008, I received an official-looking piece of mail with the address of the courthouse on the back.

When I opened up the letter it began, "Happy New Year, you are scheduled to appear . . ."

Not so happy, if you ask me. In my mind, I thought Brad Adams must have written this letter.

A short time later, I hired the white lawyer Jerry Daniels, who I knew from his helping defend my uncle, and I pled *not guilty.* The next month, however, there was another hearing, and the district attorney and my lawyer agreed that I would take the conviction open-ended and be able to ask a judge for probation.

Daniels told me he'd do his best to keep me from serving time but, again, wasn't too encouraging.

Aw, hell, I remember thinking, *I'm about to need some divine intervention.*

On the morning of my hearing, I called my grandmomma Mary, as sweet and merry as her name suggests, to let her know where I'd be for the next six to eight months. Or longer. My momma's momma, Grandmomma Mary, said she'd tell my sisters Torrie and Shavonne what was up. My second call was to Momma Doog, a cousin on my father's side of the family, who also said she was gonna pass the word on to her daughter Jackie, my cousin as well, as close as a sister to me. Momma Doog promised to keep an eye on my Crown Victoria and handle any other logistics that came up.

In her positive, practical way, Momma Doog told me, "Don't worry. We got you."

She always had my back. Always had and always would.

Help Is on the Way

As I'm walking up to the courthouse, I notice that Brad Adams is not in the group of police standing around waiting to follow me inside. But there, arms folded, glaring at me, is Sheriff Fields who comes right up and BLASTS out like a foghorn: "I hope he locks you up, Colley! I'm gonna make sure he gives you the maximum!"

Jerry Daniels tugs at my arm, giving me a look supposed to make me stay composed and we continue into the building and veer toward the courtroom. Inside it, everybody is where you'd expect—on one side is Sheriff Fields, the deputy sheriff, some more police, and the district attorney, and, on the other side, it's me and my lawyer and a beautiful, white middle-aged woman named Judy Rocker, a probation officer. Just then, the bailiff looks up as about four attractive young female friends in their early twenties file in.

If you're thinking they came to cheer me on and be character witnesses, I hate to disappoint you. They have come to the hearing because they are just nosy. And this is what counts as entertainment. It's Millen.

Actually, I'd asked my closest friends and family members *not* to come to court. Hedging my bet. The way I see it is, this might not be the time to flaunt my status as the Man in the Town, swag right and everything. If pride is gonna come before destruction, just in case, I better show my humility and my commitment to the straight and narrow.

Among this group is a friend of one of my brothers, a girl by the name of Sheree, always with an opinion, who comes over and says, "Dewayne, I'm gonna give you some talking points in case the judge asks you some questions." That isn't just nosy, it verges on not minding her own business. But I thank her just the same and listen to what she has to say. Her main points are to be sincere, talk about being a provider for my kids, and, "Don't just say you'll do better next time."

And then the judge comes in. *Mannnnnn,* the temperature all at once gets arctic cold. Judge Turner is a dead ringer for an older, scowling Donald Trump—famous at the time from *The Apprentice,* not yet president of the United States.

My lawyer, Jerry Daniels, presents his big argument about why I should get probation, talkin' about how I've never been in any real trouble, and how I was a star basketball player at Jenkins High School, and a hard working man, a valued employee of Georgia Power & Electric, and so on. The DA objects because, as he points out, "Mr. Colley is a known drug dealer and he's been arrested three times for running from the police." I sink lower in my seat, aware that this is not going well for me.

The judge practically rolls his eyes at my lawyer. That's it, I know that they are going to march me straight to lockup. And over across from me is Sheriff Fields, chomping at the bit to have his say about why I'm a menace to society. Finally, the judge looks over at the sheriff and asks, "What is your recommendation? What do you know of this guy?" and Sheriff Fields opens his mouth to respond, but all we hear is the sound of a phone ringing.

The sheriff looks down at his cell phone and then back up at the judge, explaining, "Police emergency." With that, he dashes out. In his place, the deputy sheriff rises and mumbles something about their recommendation, at which point Judge Turner asks, "Have you ever had any problem with Mr. Colley?"

The deputy sheriff shrugs and says, "No, sir, your Honor."

I look toward the heavens on high and quietly praise the Lord. But I'm not out of hell yet. I get that reality check from the impatient snarl in the judge's voice when he says, "Stand up, Mr. Colley." I see a mixture of anger and glee, a tip-off as to why he has the reputation for giving maximum sentences. Judge Turner looks directly at me as he says, "Your lawyer, Mr. Daniels, has already said why he thinks you shouldn't be incarcerated for a felony crime."

"Yes, sir, your Honor . . ." I say, not sure what's next.

"Anything you care to add?"

Suddenly, remembering Sheree's earlier suggestions to keep it as real and sincere as I can, I do just that, explaining, "Your Honor, I'm a father of two kids and I am their sole source of support. I been at Georgia Power & Electric for almost six months and I'm doin' good . . ."

The judge looks unimpressed.

Thinking fast, I quickly add, "Thing is—if you put me in jail, that's two more kids the government's gonna have to take care of."

Sometimes it's only your pride that pushes you to go for broke with the truth.

Judge Turner's scowl fades a little. The turned-down sides of his mouth straighten out—almost into a grin, but he's holding back. Looking around the courtroom, I see everybody else trying to keep from laughing.

Damn, I wonder. *What's so funny? I'm 'bout to serve eight months or more for a felony.*

Judge Turner forces his face back into a stern frown again and asks, "What's to keep you from going right back out and selling drugs if I give you a lighter sentence?"

I freeze. Sheree hadn't given me any notes for that. So I have no choice but to be even more real.

"Your Honor," I begin, pulling numbers out of thin air, "I paid fifteen hundred dollars buying the cocaine—and I only made five hundred back before I got caught by the police. Then I paid five thousand for my lawyer. I'm six thousand dollars in the hole *and* about to go to jail. So . . ." I pause, aware that you can hear a pin drop in the courtroom, and add with a nod, "I do *not* think drug dealing is for me."

My lawyer's eyes flick over at me, maybe concerned that I'm pushing it here.

Too late. I could have stopped talking but I'm on a roll like toilet paper—and my pride goads me on. I go right ahead and add, "Now I really know that crime does not pay, but you will always pay for crime!"

Before I get that last comment fully out, I notice Judge Turner's face literally turning bright red from trying so hard not to bust out laughing. But by the end of my response, he *falls out,* cracking up so bad he has to wipe his eyes. *Sho'nuff*, the whole courtroom starts to laugh in an uproar.

If I was a betting man—and unfortunately I am!—I would never have dreamt that the judge could have looked kindly on me, turning his courtroom into a damn comedy club! And, of course, the DA and everybody gunning for me were laughing the loudest.

The laughter was so *loud*, in fact, that I didn't hear Judge Turner give out the sentence.

Everyone later said it was *unheard of* from this judge—who had been on the bench for most of his seventy-something years—to show any leniency. All I knew at the time was that the entire place emptied in seconds. The only people left were me, my lawyer, and my soon-to-be probation officer. Confused, I stood up and put my hands behind my back, waiting for the bailiff, who was nowhere to be seen. I'd been prepared to go from the courtroom to prison because, well, that's just par for the course for any Black defendant in Millen, and nothing I had heard indicated otherwise.

Jerry Daniels—weathered, old, white Kountry lawyer that he was—placed his hand on my shoulder and said, "Dewayne, you are free to go." My dumbfounded expression prompted him to explain, "You got ten years' probation."

Help had shown up right on time.

Speak Right into the Storm

As you can see from my real-life scenario, when pride is all you have, sometimes it's all you need. Now, I'm not saying you should try this exact strategy and expect to get the same results. What I *am* saying is that when all you can say is, "Aw, hell!" because you are having a setback or facing obstacles you don't know how to overcome, your pride can help you speak right into the storm. Your pride lets you communicate your desired outcome. Be proud of you and your unique way of expressing yourself. When you are authentic, proudly speaking from your heart, you can touch other people's hearts or make them laugh and open up their minds.

It's true that I didn't walk out of the courthouse and snap my fingers to kick off my show business career. Many more detours, mistakes, and lessons were to come. But this was one of the most powerful demonstrations of how I could use my mouth for good. And that opened up new possibilities that would ultimately take me to the top.

You don't need to walk around giving hundred dollar bills out to the *ladeeees* like Buddy to feel pride in yourself. Then again, you gotta give Buddy credit for investing in real estate enough that he can retire and draw comfortably from his 401(k). You don't have be like Drip and finance your own rap career with money you made in the streets. Then again, you gotta give him credit for choosing to try to get out of the streets. The point is, if there is something in your life that doesn't make you proud, put your energy into what it is about you or what you have done that does make you feel good.

Your pride is like a muscle you gotta flex more often. It's a strength that keeps you grounded and pushing. It's God-given. In the Kountry, in the City, and everywhere. Use your pride. Know that it's okay if all you have is your hustle and whatever it is that makes you proud. You can change your game overnight, no hype, because I'm here to tell you that with the will to win, an ability to grind, and some help along the way, anything is possible.

CHAPTER 2

KOUNTRY TOWN

Live Your Truth

What if I told you right now that you had buried treasure in your backyard? Or, if you don't have a backyard, what if I told you that you had a valuable property deed tucked away somewhere that you've ignored for too long?

You probably wouldn't believe me either way.

Yeah, I might be suspicious, too—except I already believe that everything we learn from the world that raised us, everything we loved and hated, can be turned into gold. Of course, I'm not saying you should go dig holes in the ground outside or run around opening drawers and cleaning out your closets. I'm just suggesting that when you choose to own the truth of where you come from—good, bad, or in between—it will remind you of who you are and help guide you to where you're going.

Where you come from gives you your starting place in the world, like a compass setting. It's your history, your family's history. It's your inheritance of talents, habits, and traits, for better and for worse, and the blessings and curses given to you when you were born. It's the environment that could have held you back or pushed you. It's all of that. You are not supposed to stay there for life. You are supposed to grow up, leave the nest so you can test your wings, and go into the wider world, learn more lessons, multiply, and prosper.

But not everyone does. They get stuck. They lose their drive and forget their dreams and ambitions. They forget to see possibility for themselves. Maybe they never could.

If you want to understand your superpowers and how to put them to use, pay attention to the value of *living your truth*. You'll be relieved that you don't have to hide from your humble beginnings anymore. You also don't have to apologize for privileges, either.

The best part of living your truth and not trying to be someone you aren't, or pretending to be from somewhere you've never been is, *you stop caring what other people think*. That is a power move. Then you get to be the Real One, too. You'll find what I have found—that God blesses the real and the Devil blesses the fake.

People laugh when I tell them that where I come from, plain and simple, was *the mud*. No joke. "Straight out the mud" is not an exaggeration. Now it's a slogan. But growing up in the Georgia mud was no picnic. I had to learn to live it before I could finally leave it.

No hype. Just being real.

In the Mud

Here's the truth: *My momma was a playa, my daddy was a playa. So what that make me? A playa from the Himalayas!* (Shout out to Martin Lawrence, who I quoted in one of my early viral rap hits.)

A basic reality is that we all arrive in this world with inherited blessings and curses. When you live that truth, you can choose to accept the good and do something to escape the bad.

For the first ten years of my life, I grew up as a Coney—same as my momma, Melissa, and my sisters. My daddy, Vincent "Skip" Colley, the big Man in the Town when I was growing up, a playa and a hustler, wasn't much in the picture in the early years. He'd come around now and then, but he and Momma weren't together. On the Coney side, I was the youngest of Momma's three kids, and the only boy. On the Colley side, I was the oldest of my father's seven kids, two girls and five boys. Eventually, circumstances being what they were, Daddy tried to make up for lost time and wanted me to have his last name like my brothers, who had different mommas. So, later on, I agreed and went from being Coney to Colley overnight.

At school, I was still alphabetically in the same spot, aside from a switch of the *n* for two *ll*s. *Nuthin* much changed, but deep down I had mixed feelings. We are taught in the Bible to honor our father and our mother, but it doesn't say that you have to love your parents or pretend that they are perfect all the time. The truth is that my relationship with my pop was complicated.

On an up note, being known as the firstborn son of Skip Colley gave me a reputation before I earned it—like I was supposed to step into his shoes one day. Daddy had presence. He carried himself as someone important. You could see it in how he walked—like he had places to go and people to see. You could tell by how the ladies fluffed their feathers and came around when they saw him pull up. He had the Kountry cool alright, driving a big flashy car that went along with his role as the boss of his business. But, as I later learned, he broke a couple of the cardinal rules for hustling—such as remembering to keep a low profile and never getting high on your own supply. Those are things Drip would have warned him about.

The real ace up my daddy's sleeve was that he was always funny. With a devilish twinkle in his eye, he had you laughing before he said anything. And that goes for my uncles who *coulda* formed a Kountry barbershop of comedy. For that matter, most of the Colleys and the Coneys have a sense of humor. Family get-togethers were so dang funny, we *coulda* sold tickets. Especially when the grown folks were drinking. Back when I was in diapers, I didn't understand a word of what they said, but I heard the music and the rhythm of joke—and storytelling—and laughed along with the adults.

My daddy could cut it up with the best of them. But he was heart-attack serious when he needed to be and he was good at his business. Now, for a long time I didn't know what that business was—which was strange because as far back as Head Start, I knew pretty much every-thing else that was goin' down in the town. All I really knew, unfortu-nately, was that even though Pops might be carrying some paper on him, enough to spare at times, his obligations were spread thin, and we weren't at the top of the list.

There were certain occasions when he was nowhere to be found. Growing up, I assumed he was out of town, doing whatever he did to make money. Later on, I found out he was in Millen the whole time, just hiding from all his kids and baby mamas. But he'd slip up and go to the store and you'd be at the store, too, and you'd catch him running out the door to his car, looking back and trying to blend in with the pavement, and you'd wonder, *Was that Daddy?* Later, when I did track him down I'd ask, "Did I just see you at the store the other day?"

"Naw, son, uh that wasn't me . . . Uh . . . Store? What store?"

"Daddy, I was in the car right behind you."

Why hide from your kids? Made no sense until I was older. He hid because he had gone broke at that moment. Later he changed but he was never a nine-to-five worker who came home and sat down to dinner with his kids. He wasn't a go-camping-and-fishing-on-the-weekends or help-you-with-your-homework type of father, either. So he became what you might call a money dad. And he wasn't always so good at that.

Happens in every kind of town and city. Being a provider would be expected from all dads. That's a given. But there is more to being a father. Knowing your kids, being there for them, honestly, that's worth more than money. As a parent today, spending time with my children is at the top of my priority list. That said, if you can't be in their lives, you can be a money dad and a provider. Just know that, if you go broke, you may have to hide from your kids.

The part that most bothered me was that there was nobody helping Momma. Nobody. Not the men who were fathers of her children, not really anyone in her family, not any of the men who came to be with her and who would leave her something after they did. Momma never complained or blamed, but I saw how the struggle was all on her. She did it with a smile—whatever she had to do to give us a roof over our heads, feed and dress us. All on her own.

Momma was one of the most beautiful women ever to come out of Millen, Georgia, and she was smart, kind, good-hearted, and always real. Despite the challenges, *mannnnnn*, Melissa Coney made it look easy. She had style with a capital *S*. She could rub two dimes together and—*poof*—look like a thousand bucks, like a fashion model right there in the Kountry. Between whatever she could get from the Buddy-type men who came around and a small amount of money from some kind of government check, Momma kept us going, in spite of many obstacles.

Nobody on either the Coney or Colley sides of the family ever had anything like the $20,000 needed to put a down payment on a home. Nobody had the credit to get loans, either. That meant we moved a lot. Momma made it an adventure. Like an extended camping trip. In hindsight, I realize this helped me adapt to having a career on the road and learn to travel light.

Growing up in Millen, the first place where we lived was in my grandmomma's house—a three-bedroom modest home. It wasn't much, I'm not gonna lie. Later on, we moved into a single-wide tin-can trailer owned by my grandmomma Mary that sat right next to the train tracks. You'd get numb with the cold in winter and hotter than hell in the summer. To this day, I have PTSD from the noise and the shaking whenever a train passed by. My sisters and I got to where we couldn't go to sleep until the first train came rattling through at around 11:00 p.m. Once we heard the first train whistle blow, we fell asleep *right away*. We had conditioned ourselves to wait so we wouldn't get rudely yanked out of sleep by the noise. We qualified early on for government housing—a two-bedroom unit in a one-story duplex. That's what they call "the projects" in Millen.

During our summers in Atlanta with family on the Coney side, we stayed in the City projects, basically a trailer park. It wasn't a concrete jungle ghetto like on TV but making do was a lot *harsher* than in the small town. Not only that, but in the City, the more sophisticated people would make remarks and look down on you because you were poor and had *nuthin*. The truth? I *hated* that. In the Kountry, poor was still poor, but maybe because it was simpler, the experience was more tolerable. You could hang out at someone else's place and relax until you could figure out the rent. Some folks don't even realize they are poor in the Kountry.

Somehow, I figured it out young. Before I could put words to it, the truth came to me that poverty is a curse. In time, I understood that a lot of folks naturally try to escape that realization—with drugs, alcohol, sex, or however they can—if only to forget their worries for a minute.

In the Kountry, no surprise, where there's not much to do, drinking is a popular pastime. For one thing, nobody needs to impress anyone with expensive alcohol, so the liquor's cheaper. And for another thing, everywhere you need to go is "over yonder" and you can walk places without drinking and driving.

Nobody ever needed an excuse to drink, but it usually started with someone stopping by and saying, "Well, Melissa, why not? It's my birthday!" Momma, being real, would say, "Yo birthday come and gone." But then she'd smile and say it was *somebody's* birthday soon, why not celebrate ahead of time?

I was impressed at how many excuses grown folks would invent as reasons to sit down, drink, play cards, smoke, and whatnot—everything from "I got a job" to "I lost a job" to "It's Friday!" to "Well, it's not Sunday." Before long, there would be a rip-roaring card game going on, no plans for making real food, and nothing in the refrigerator.

I'm not much more than a tiny tot and I'm watching everybody carrying on and I do *not* believe it. I'm just standing there lookin' at

Momma and everyone, scratching my head. Until finally I let loose with a really *loud* statement of fact: "Hey! Don't y'all see? We're *poor*!"

Everything stops. You can hear a pin drop. Everyone looks at Momma and then back at me and then back at their cards.

Next thing, somebody says something like, "Well, hell, I'll drink to that," and everybody falls out laughing like no tomorrow. All I can think is that I'm gonna have to get money on my own—the truth I choose to live.

There was usually that one person in a family gathering who'd get the drunkest and the funniest. My auntie Ruby was often that relative. Not just funny from being high, Ruby had mad comedy skills. She put on an advanced class in timing, double takes, and hitting a punch line like a race car stopping on a dime. She could mimic voices and act out different characters. She was *funnnnnyyyy!*

My momma wasn't a cutup or show-off. But she knew good comedy when she heard it. Getting her to laugh hard was a prize. She didn't laugh at just anybody. I could see, young as I was, that in the time when Skip and Melissa were originally together, he must have had a special gift he used to get her interested. His was the kind of humor that sneaks up on you and swallows you like a wave until you can't stop laughing. He had a half-serious, half-mischievous twinkle that was disarming. You might not even know he was joking. The other thing about my pops Skip that I noticed as a little child, before I knew how he made a living, was that he had a boss mentality—meaning he could laugh with the best of them but most of the time he didn't party too hard. That is, unless he was in pursuit of a woman. They were his weakness, his escape, especially crazy women, and they could mess with his business and his money. Then he'd look for another escape and sample the goods he had for selling—another pitfall every hustler ought to know.

The possibility of a curse that I couldn't name hung over me. At different points, I got some specifics when my momma and daddy admitted that addiction was the biggest pitfall to be avoided. The way they told it, the minute you let down your guard, it would take hold of you and *not* let you go. Both of them had given in and gotten high for the first time when they were twenty-two years old.

That's it, I told myself, *I am never gonna drink a drop of alcohol or smoke one hit of weed. Not only that but—I GOTTA make this money before the addiction curse kicks in.*

I believed having a better life was possible because I'd been shown the light. Literally. Shining bright on the television set and demonstrated by a handful of characters I saw on the TV. Thanks to them, I not only wanted to win and would rather die than lose, but I believed the truth that if they could do it, so could I.

Kountry Dreamin'

I don't know where I'd be today without cable. No hype. Momma would be late on all kinds of bills, we couldn't eat no pork chops, and we'd come close to having the lights turned off but somehow she kept enough juice in the line and the poor man's cable turned on. The VCR was my lifeline into another world. I got my own Head Start at home watching '80s and '90s movies and TV shows like *Pretty Woman, Purple Rain, The Fresh Prince of Bel-Air, Martin,* and *A Different World.*

If Richard Gere could use his money to get a woman off the streets and then they could fall in love, too, why couldn't I eventually do something like that? If Prince could write his own ticket to fame and fortune, it could be done. Above all, it was Eddie Murphy who planted the seeds of possibility for me. The fact that he was funny AND the biggest box office movie star in the world was an example of him using his God-given gifts to make money and get the girls like in *Boomerang*. I knew that film backward and forward. But what I loved most was how through his roles he found a way to outsmart everyone to make it big.

Trading Places was proof that you could start poor but not get stuck there. The characters in *Coming to America* were more real to me than my own family. I watched the movie so many times I could recite the lines. Still can. I'd sit there and watch how Arsenio Hall took an old raggedy apartment and transformed it into a royal bachelor pad. *Mannnnnn,* I couldn't wait to have some money to turn the rat-hole places where we lived into luxury homes. What really showed me the definition of someone being rich for real was the part in *Coming to America* when Eddie Murphy gave money to the homeless people.

That, more than anything, motivated me to keep believing I could do so well one day that I could help people who were cursed by poverty and stuck in struggle. Once I set that in front of me, it was true because I'd seen someone else do it—even if they weren't really real.

Very few people ever encouraged me. Not because of me but because of their own low expectations. And that was the worst part of growing up in a Kountry town—feeling like you must be fooling yourself because you *see* something that nobody else can see.

Living my truth meant I had to learn not to care about what other people thought or said. I had to learn to appreciate all the lessons I was being given by the Kountry characters I knew and loved, as well as the ones I didn't care much for. I had to learn that there was nothing wrong with the things that I wanted and to never, ever limit myself.

I've also had to remind myself of one of the realest blessings of being born Kountry, and, in particular, where I come from. Kountry people, even the small-minded ones, are mostly loving and basically warmhearted. They are not mean. They are trusting as can be. Back when I grew up, folks didn't lock their doors. *Nuthin* much to steal. If you needed a place to stay, folks would find space. Why wouldn't they? They were not doing much of anything anyway.

Kountry soul—the sharing of good vibes—is an abundant commodity that's good for the world and makes you rich in every sense of the word.

It's Never Too Late to Reset Your GPS

There are places like Millen everywhere. Folks who feel stuck can be Black/white/brown/you-name-it. In hard times, they feel like everything's working against them. The old choices for a regular legit job have been vanishing for years. Big employers have been closing down many of their operations, sending skilled jobs overseas or replacing skilled workers with robots. That's real.

There are places up North, out West, and in all directions, even in the cities, where people don't feel attached to where they come from— like they landed there by accident and would go anywhere else if they could. It's no secret.

But wait. All is not lost. Help is on the way.

When you choose to live your truth, as Drip would tell you, that's the first step to removing the mental shackles of limitation. You don't have to apologize for choosing to improve your situation. When someone decides they think you don't belong in nicer places, you just use Drip's words: "Yuh, wherever my feet go, I go." Live the truth of your juice and, like Drip, tell anyone who wants to push you out, "Yuh, I'm the hottest in the Citeeee!" Then give 'em that look that says, "Aw, you know you want me."

Now Buddy's a good example of a guy who makes no apologies. You can hear it in the familiar way he talks to a girl on the street he's never met. "Hey, bebee, little dahlin' . . . " And he flashes that money roll. He's so honest about who he is that he talks about himself in the third person, like, "You know, Buddy living his truth is helping other people see their truth. Ya see, I'm teachin' these young'uns that if a man handles his business, there won't be no room for Buddy in his woman's life. I am a public servant."

My point is, you were born to be somebody. Own that. You don't have to feel stuck. You also don't have to listen to what everyone else tells you is or is not possible for you. When you take the time to quiet your mind and think back to the world that shaped you, I bet you might be able to see a truth about the blessings and the curses you were given at the start. You most likely will be reminded of an early truth about the destination you wanted for yourself and the people you care about most. It's never too late to reset your GPS.

Just remember that where you begin doesn't have to be where you end up. I am a shining example of that! When you live the truth of where you come from, you'll be reminded of who you really are, deep down, and who you were always meant to be.

CHAPTER 3

FLOWER CHILD

Don't Confuse Knowledge with Wisdom

As a hustler—and don't forget everybody's got a hustle—you're probably in a hurry to gain as much knowledge as you can, as fast as you can. *Nuthin* wrong with that. *Except* . . . if you don't also learn how to use the knowledge *wisely,* you'll wind up getting stuck in neutral without the tools to move forward.

That was me at many different stages of my life. Finding *knowledge* was never a problem, but I often lacked the *wisdom* to use it. If you pay attention, listen more than you speak, and use your deep, inner powers of observation, there is an avalanche of information at your fingertips. The hitch is that, when you aren't ready for that knowledge, it will go to waste because you don't yet have the wisdom to put it to use. Or, worse, knowledge that you don't really understand can be dangerous.

Learning how not to confuse knowledge with wisdom will help you see that both are important but they're not the same thing. Sometimes you will have worldly knowledge without spiritual wisdom. That's trouble. Sometimes practical knowledge is necessary. Sometimes being so head smart weighs you down and prevents you from connecting to your instincts. Too much knowledge can make you overthink what you are doing and fall into the trap of "paralysis by analysis."

Knowledge can look foolish to wisdom. Sure, a lot of us use the words to mean more or less the same thing. And the differences can be subtle. For example, when I was young, I had a scary amount of knowledge about adult problems without the wisdom of *how* to solve the problems. Knowledge will give you the "what" of a problem. Wisdom will give you the "how" and the "when," the "where" and the "why."

In the world of sports, as another example, Michael Jordan and Phil Jackson each have amazing basketball knowledge. If they had a baby together, its name would be Wisdom. Phil understands the "how" of all the moving pieces and Michael, the team leader, makes it happen on the court. Knowledge (skills) will give you an edge, but wisdom wins every time.

Everybody right now has information overload. There's misinformation and disinformation. That's not always knowledge. It could be fancy gossip. Real knowledge that you learn, absorb, understand, and put to use is essential. But if you are just going to store it in your brain, that's like owning a fleet of Ferraris and not having your driver's license yet.

The danger of gaining knowledge without wisdom must be an important lesson because it's just about the first story in the Bible—right there in Genesis with Adam and Eve in the Garden of Eden. God tells Adam that they can have whatever they want to eat anywhere in the whole garden—with one exception. Whatever you do, Adam is told, do *not* eat from the Tree of Knowledge of Good and Evil. A lot of people blame Eve for tempting Adam to eat the apple after she was persuaded to do so by Satan. But Eve is innocent. God never told the rules to her. Satan whispered in her ear to get her to tempt Adam. So Satan is punished by having to slither around on his belly as a snake. That doesn't clear Adam because he should have listened to God. If it was David out in the fields watching his sheep, he would have said, "Oh, no, I ain't gonna eat that apple," and passed on the message to Eve.

But Adam doesn't have the wisdom to know the consequences of breaking the rules. Once they eat the forbidden fruit they immediately realize they are buck naked—and you know what happens next. Of course, God is mad because Adam ignored the rules, didn't even bother telling Eve, and then blamed her for causing them to gain knowledge before they were ready.

My interpretation is that God would have eventually let them eat from the Tree of Knowledge of Good and Evil once they had cultivated wisdom. The moral of the story is, when your Higher Power sends you a message, listen to it! That's the first step on the road to growing up and becoming wise.

Born Grown

Anyone who remembers me as a little kid will testify that I was born grown. My aunties and uncles—on both Colley and Coney sides—*still* use any chance they get to talk my ear off about how none of the adults were willing to take care of me. They did *not* like me. If my momma needed a break and tried to get somebody—anybody—to take me for an hour or so, to babysit, they'd all tell her, "Nah, Melissa, that chile is too grown up!"

They'd say it was creepy because I could see stuff about them and say things I was not supposed to know.

My powers of observation had set in early and if something didn't make sense, I'd speak up. So . . . I was mouthy. *Real* mouthy. Take the situation with one of my Coney uncles, my momma's brother Cleave. Somehow, some kind of way, he got to shack up with some of the finest ladies in Millen. *White* ladies, too. *Well-to-do white* ladies.

Now, this uncle worked for my pops, meaning he had some money, but not a lot. He had some serious swag, though—a big ole shiny gold tooth, just one, and a smile that would *not* stop. He wasn't too flashy but he drove his late '80s model Oldsmobile Cutlass Supreme—with the high-riding back end and sporty, low-riding front hood—like he was King of the Road. That Cutlass Supreme was his big horse in the Kountry and the ladies couldn't get enough of him.

Made no sense to me. I tried to listen when he talked to the women to hear how he cast a spell over them, but he'd lean in so close, I could never hear the actual words he used. All I knew is that he stayed with a woman named Christie who was white and had money.

Picture this: One day, when I am only like five and a half, I just blurt out to my uncle, "How'd yo Black ass get such a fine white woman like that?"

My uncle shakes his head. "Did you say what I think you said, boy?"

I'm not even six years old and I know enough to point out how Christie is an educated woman and my uncle didn't even finish high school. I had to know his angle. What did he say to her? "C'mon, what's the magic words you use?" I ask.

"You wanna know my secret?" my uncle comes back. He starts to tell me and then says, "Nah, you too young."

"You jes said I was too grown. Make up yo mind!"

My uncle decides to tell me if I promise to keep his secret. He says that you have to treat a woman like a queen: Always talk to her sweet, tell her no other woman can compete with her, and, always, let her know you'd do anything for her to feel good.

"Like what?"

You probably see where this is going. I wanted this knowledge and it would be of use later on. At the time, though, he was going to give me a charm that I wasn't ready to use.

"Worship the ground she walk on." My uncle saw me looking confused, so he explained, "Kiss her feet."

"That's it? The whole secret?"

"Not just kiss 'em," he said, "but you have to rub up on her feet, too. And take yo time. That's the *real* secret. No woman wanna *wham, bam, thank you, ma'am.*"

I was suspicious. He had to be making all that up. "Her feet? Don't it tickle?"

Baby playa that I was, one night when Uncle Cleave brought Christie to my momma's house, I had a chance to test the technique.

My momma, my uncles, and some friends were in the kitchen playing cards and drinking gin and juice, while I was on the sofa with—guess who?—Christie. She had her shoes off! She had a blanket over her and I grabbed a pillow, laid down with my head near her feet, and positioned myself so I could let my hand graze a toe or two. At one point, I went for it and began to massage her feet with the gentle and firm grip of a soon to be six-year-old. She turned and looked at me, surprised, but then turned back to the TV—as if she could see I was grown enough to know what I was doing.

My uncle's instruction had stayed with me. I took my time to feel her toes, ankles, the back of her heels, and the bottoms and tops of her

41

two, dainty pink feet. They were silky smooth. Like laying my cheek on heavenly pillows. After a good half hour, Uncle Cleave got up from the card table and came into the living room, ready to go, and said, "I'ma holla at you, nephew."

For a minute, I felt bitter, like he was walking out the door with my woman.

This was a case of me gaining knowledge before I was ready to use it wisely. But it *sho'nuff* worked.

In time, fortunately, I figured out some wisdom about the importance of how you make people feel. When I was ready, I finally understood what all those women saw in him. That knowledge came from noticing how the men in my family, and the women, too, Colleys and Coneys, used their charisma, swag, and sense of humor to draw people in like bees to honey. Sauce ran in the family.

When you treat everyone around you like a queen or king, you make them feel wonderful. Everyone can practice techniques for having swag or being popular but only a wise person knows that it's not how cool or special you are—it's how cool and special everyone around you gets to feel.

And that's some Kountry wisdom you can take to the bank.

Seek Your Sign

Because of the adult problems going on around me, I needed at least some knowledge as a child to try to make sense of everything. Sometimes all I had to do was ask blunt questions and I'd get answers. But finding wisdom was another story. Deep down in my spirit, I wanted the wisdom of knowingness—a reassurance that life could get better. Of course, I believed in God but He seemed far away at times. Like I was sending out an SOS that was too small to be heard. All I wanted was a signal, a sign, sent back to me.

At the different churches we attended, I'd hear about God sending signs and even talking to certain chosen ones when times were hard. In Sunday School, I learned that God spoke to Noah and said it was time to build an ark because a giant flood was coming. God even made a bush light on fire to get the attention of Moses so He could give him instructions for leading the people to the Promised Land. When I heard that God sent signs, wonders, and miracles to the apostles of Jesus, sometimes when they didn't expect to receive anything, I figured there was a chance I could get a sign, too.

Grown folks in the Kountry would also talk about what some might call superstitions but were signs being sent to them—like how when a bird flies in the house, it's a sign that bad luck is about to happen or how somebody heard a voice speaking lucky numbers that they used to win a lottery. That was proof right there I was gonna get some kind of message.

Everywhere I went, I looked high and low for my sign. Nothing flashed before me. Nothing spoke to me. This went on for weeks. Then, one blazing-hot, humid Kountry summer day, all of a sudden, a gooooood, relaxed, contented feeling came over me. It was a taste, a hint, of knowingness—like a tiny light bulb lit up with a small *dingggg* sound. I stopped cold, looked up at the sky, and said—out loud but in a slight whisper—"Me and God got a special relationship."

This is a few months before my sixth birthday, maybe in August or September.

The very next day, I notice a tall, skinny, awkward sunflower in my Great-Grandmomma Emma's yard. Never saw it before. The sunflower is growing up out of a little clay pot next to a garden patch somebody must've planted at one time near the front porch. The strange thing is that sunflower season has already passed. It only lasts ten days or so in July and now it's about to be peanut harvest season. Don't ask how I know but I do. Maybe it's my imagination but, *sho'nuff,* the sunflower seems to be watching me. From one angle, it has its chocolate-brown face turned to me as I come out of the house. From another angle, it's looking at me sideways, turned to the street, when I start to leave. *Could a flower really be watching me?*

Could this be my sign?

Well, maybe, if God is real, I tell myself, *this could be it!* So I wait for the right moment, when no one is around, just me out in the front yard. My momma, great-grandmomma Emma, and auntie Ruby are inside fanning themselves and staying out of the morning heat.

Making no sudden movement, I tiptoe slowly up close to the sunflower and I say, "Talk to me."

Nothing. Not even a flutter of a yellow petal.

"Talk to me," I repeat, adding, "I won't tell nobody."

Nothing. Wait! Maybe, but I can't really tell, I see the sunflower do an itty-bitty sway in the wind. Yeah, I'm not sure about that. So, just in case, I fold my arms with determination and say one last time, "I *know* you can talk."

Next thing that happens is the flower TALKS TO ME! The flower not only curls over and bends all the way down to the ground but it talks with the sound of a clown whistle going low—like a cartoon when the clown slides down a pole. Then the flower lifts right back up, straight and tall, and the clown whistle sound this time was like the clown is sliding back up a pole. The flower just BOWED TO ME AND SAID HELLO IN PLANT LANGUAGE!

I'm so happy and so stunned! I know right then that this is a sign from God that He is with me. I know how I promised not to tell nobody but I can't help myself. This is something supernatural and I fly up the steps and call into the living room, "I got this flower. It just talk to me! I got a sign!"

I say to the side, to the sunflower, "I know I told you I won't tell nobody but this is it, I'm not gonna tell nobody ELSE."

Inside, Momma, Great-Grandmomma Emma, and Auntie Ruby try to wave me away. Great-Grandmomma Emma, a devout church-goer, warns my momma that this is what happens when you don't go to church enough. "A talking flower? A sign? Lawd have mercy."

"It's real," I insist. "Y'all come out. Look, look! Hurry!"

I could have sworn that the magic flower had turned my way completely and was following our conversation.

Clearly, none of the women believed me, but I was so serious they got up and came fast outside, down to where the sunflower stood looking a little wilted in the humidity.

"Go ahead," I said. "You can talk to the flower and get an answer!"

The three of them—in their span of ages ranging from twenties to sixties—shot each other embarrassed looks for letting a six-year-old trick them into talking to a flower.

They tried. I'll give them that. But they got no response.

I went over and talked to the flower, all friendly, saying, "Talk to them, too, like you talked to me. That way they'll know I'm tellin' the truth."

Nothing. Not a peep. Not a dingggg.

Aunt Ruby, muttering about me having crazy ideas in my head, led the three of them back into the house. Momma turned back for a last

45

look at the sunflower, giving it one more chance. She wanted to believe like I did. But the sunflower stood there, as lonely and awkward as before, nothing magical about it for anyone but me.

No matter what hardships came next, that was the moment that changed my life for the better. I felt powerful. Flower power! That made me a flower child, I guess.

Strange as it may seem, real wisdom came alive for me after that. To this day, I can feel the love and encouragement that warmed me when the flower bent down and spoke to me. It was also the beginning of being able to see the difference between knowledge and wisdom. Knowledge came with a responsibility and an acceptance that maybe I was too grown-up for my age. That's how it was gonna be, I realized, but wisdom told me that I'd be given the right lessons to put that knowledge to use.

Wisdom is a different kind of knowingness—sacred, special, and custom-made for you, your life, and the people you love. No matter what anyone else said to convince me otherwise, I knew that God—whoever you call the one who made the sky blue and the wind blow—was there for me. From that point on I accepted that there was a plan and a purpose for me and that we didn't have to be in the mud forever.

That didn't mean it was all gonna be easy. Knowledge made that clear. And so did wisdom.

The Lesson of How *Not* to Be

Knowledge can keep you safe but can also be dangerous to your peace of mind. When you put your powers of observation to work, you can't ignore the negatives that exist in this world. It's upsetting when you *know* there is injustice, yet you think there's *nuthin* you can do to change it.

In the Kountry and in the City, I watched people suffer from the double curse of poverty *and* racism. Hard to pretend that the world is a fair place. In our situation, it always bothered me knowing my pops had some money but was not making the choice (or was not able) to look out for Momma and us. Why? The question—*why we struggling so hard?*—burned a hole inside me. Help might have been on the way, eventually, but it was moving too slow.

My conclusion was that I was gonna have to get powerful wisdom about *how to get me some money.* Once I had paper of my own, I was sure, our problems would disappear. That thought gave me courage in those times when we barely had anything to eat, while Pops was out there with a nice car, a pocket full of money, lookin' fly and not stopping by to help us out.

The silver-lining lesson I learned from my pops Skip of those years was how *not* to be. At the least, I made a promise that no matter how many children I had one day—you can call me a prophet—my baby mamas would get help from me. I didn't have the exact knowledge of what my mother had to do in return for the men who came around and gave her money when they left. But I hated how down she seemed to feel afterward.

Momma was always real, no matter what, and made no apologies about trying to forget her sorrows, even if it meant letting the regular card games in the kitchen go late and losing track of the time. Me, being real, too, I took on the role of trying to remind her that there needed to be less card playing and more sitting down at a decent hour to eat food that stuck to our bones. Momma knew I was right but found ways to ignore my subtle hints.

One night, after a game had started late and gone on for hours, with no mention of meal preparation, I gave up trying to be subtle. I walked over and stood there with sad eyes, first, holding my skinny empty stomach, then pantomiming imaginary food going into my open mouth.

Momma didn't even look up. Still too subtle. Finally, I walked over to the other side of the table, waved my arms, interrupting the game in progress, and said, "Hey, I understand y'all playing cards, but far as I can tell, ain't no food in the house."

Momma stared at me quick and, under her breath, said, "I'm 'bout to win. I'll get you somethin' after the next hand." She proceeded to smile in an extra-loving way and to speak with more volume, saying, "Y'all can eat chips if you wait, just this one time."

"Chips?! I don't want no chips. I want some meat!"

Everyone started to laugh. Momma rolled her eyes, trying to shoo me out of there.

I grumbled like an old man, then turned back and said, "Man, listen, the ace of clubs *and* the ace of hearts you got in your hand, waiting on the ace of diamonds will not get food in here and the refrigerator don't fill itself!"

That was one of those times when somebody probably made a comment about me being too grown. "Melissa, I tole you. It's unnatural."

I didn't think it was unnatural. Knowledge, common sense, told me that having structure was important. Momma knew that as well. And just like other times, for a while she went back to the rules of making sure we had an evening meal and a set bedtime. But then something would happen—no money, no car, a bad day, a card game that went too late, and it was back to chips.

Now and then I overdid my effort to communicate my message.

One time we were at the grocery store and I tried to get myself adopted by families with shopping carts full of food. Momma, trying to keep from laughing, said, "I apologize for my son Dewayne. He look scrawny but he can eat y'all outa house and home. We feed him plenty. Y'all don't want him."

She took me by the hand, pretending to be mad, and then *cracked up*.

If I could make her laugh, in spite of our troubles, in spite of herself, that was a prize for me. I could read her, too, like when Mr. Melvin was over, and she was going to pay him extra attention. She only had to glance at me and I knew not to be underfoot. She was not weak, not soft in the least. Momma could be gangsta all the way when necessary—when pushed to it.

Only once do I remember a man putting his hands on her. Then I saw a side of Melissa Coney, and of me, I'd never seen before. As soon as he smacked her, I jumped on his back and Momma hauled off and began punching him. He weaseled out the door before anyone got seriously hurt. By then, I had found an edge—thanks to the knowledge I gained from our time living in the City.

Learn When to Roar

My reputation in the classroom was set at an early age. Teachers appreciated that I had knowledge above my years and I made good grades most of the time—mostly As and Bs. If I fell off and got a C or two, I knew how to work hard and bring my grade up. Teachers would also always make exceptions for me because I could keep everyone entertained. I was like a helpful class clown. My hustle worked there. The only problem at school was that, compared to Kountry kids my age, I was on the small side.

Trust me, size matters.

Outside during recess, *mannnnnn,* it was a war zone. On top of being scrawny, I was a flower child who didn't like to fight. But I would fight if I had to. The worst, most vicious, and ferocious bullies would try to take my snack or lunch or anything new I might have of value on me. Worse, these bullies were all *girls*! They were elementary school female gangstas! There was a girl named Pam, another named Ashley, and then there was Kim—who busted my lip one day. The worst was DeCaré. She was a relentless ringleader who took pleasure in finding new ways to jump me, and take my snacks and my stuff after giving me a good beating. If not for a big kid named JJ Graham—who'd step in now and then to help, in return for me giving him my snacks *before* the girls stole them—I would have been even worse off.

There was no wisdom available. "Turn the other cheek" worked for Jesus but not for me. If I couldn't find any wisdom, I'd settle for knowledge. An angle. In Atlanta, where we spent the summer and part of the next school year in the fall, Strategy became my middle name. This was around the time my friends in the City first started calling me Kountry—not because of how I acted but because of how I talked.

"Like y'all don't have an accent?" I'd shoot back. After all, Atlanta was still the South. I learned to sharpen the edge of my comebacks.

I also learned to be unapologetic. My sisters adapted differently. Torrie would get quiet, and avoid conflict; Shavonne adopted the tougher City ways, but more as a people pleaser who went along with the ringleaders. My approach was not to be intimidated and not to be too friendly, either. My swag became unapologetic. Didn't always work and sometimes I'd get tested. But most of the time, I learned, if you act like a lion and roar loud enough, no one wants to find out how sharp your claws really are. Now that's more than knowledge. Wisdom teaches you *restraint*.

Few people have the wisdom to trust restraint. I'm not talking about avoiding conflict completely. I'm talking about being wise enough to know when and where to be unapologetic. Restraint teaches you that you can be a lion without apology but not all the time. You can learn when to go all out and when to hold back.

The City gave me knowledge of how to hustle with intensity—as in, never standing still, learning to move fast, and not wasting energy or time. For instance, one Sunday a church was giving away whole cheesecakes and everybody who wanted one had to get in one of two lines, either on a hilly street or on another street. It occurred to me, after waiting in line for twenty-five minutes or more, that if I could run down to Momma, give her the cheesecake, and then race around to the second line and hurry up the hill, I could get her a second cheesecake. One cake per household was the rule. And knowing that supplies were getting low, I had to really speed up that second hill to get there in time before everything shut down.

"One per family," the man said, recognizing me from the other line.

I didn't budge, argue, or try to explain.

The man glared at me as I caught my breath. With my newfound attitude, I just stared back at him.

After several seconds, the man gave in, grumbling a little, and let me have the second cheesecake.

"Thank you, sir! God bless you!" I said, down-home Kountry style, before speeding off, back down the hill. The victory reminded me you can sometimes get what you want without speaking too many words. Also, I had defied a rule, developed a strategy, and it paid off. That's a dangerous piece of knowledge because rule breaking can become addictive. But it was more than worth it. Momma (who may never have had cheesecake in her life before that day) said, "Mmmmm, best I ever tasted, baby." She loved the second cheesecake even more.

In Atlanta, I was exposed to everything that was new. In the summer of 1994, at six-and-a-half, I became a die-hard 2Pac fan. True. The song "Keep Ya Head Up" played in the streets everywhere I went. It had that hooky melody and a sample from the 1970 record *O-o-h Child* by the Five Stairsteps, as 2Pac told us to stay up because "things are gonna get easier." He rapped about young men having babies and leaving mothers to be fathers, too. He rhymed about his dreams to be an emcee and act in the movies, giving me thoughts of my own possibilities. The question was planted in the soil of my imagination—could I be a rapper and become famous one day, too? Before long, I started to freestyle everywhere I went. My rhymes, though, may have left something to be desired—*I pulled the trigger and I shot that n******! But you gotta start somewhere!

Living in the City proved to me that I was right to believe help was on the way if I did my part. The proof was watching rich Black folk in Atlanta living legit lives. I saw the bigger houses and finer cars and kept those images for inspiration. There were Black businessmen in tailored suits carrying briefcases with beautiful, finely dressed Black ladies, their arms full of shopping bags filled with Lord-knows-what-all clothes and shoes. In their picture-perfect lives, they called taxis that came right away and picked them up, along with their well-behaved children, who wore the latest matching baggy sweats, hoodies, and sneakers.

Even at school, where kids in my class may have been poor like us, they all seemed to have a City confidence that showed me how I could

carry myself, too. It wasn't just how they walked, but how they talked—
with one cussword after the next. Sounded good to me! It didn't take
long for me to add several choice cusswords to my verbal arsenal.

Deep down, I was still a Kountry child. Ahhh, but my new City
swag gave me a tough edge. A feeling of power. By the time we returned to Millen, a couple months into second grade, I even felt fear-
less.

First day out at recess, I saw the girl gang come walkin' up, led by
DeCaré, who was taking her time, rolling up her sleeves, and showing
off to the others.

Instead of waiting for them to make a move, I stepped right up and
called out the ringleader. "DeCaré!"

She folded her arms, chewed her gum, rolled her eyes. Like, "What?"

"You try that shit this year you tried last year, I'm gonna beat yo
mutherf**kin' *ass!*"

DeCaré was confused. She looked down, avoiding my eyes.

I took two more steps closer and looked at the others. "Y'all wanna
try me now? I'ma tear y'all f**kin' *ass* up! *All the way up.*" They ex-
changed glances and stepped back, confused and surprised at me cussing like that. "Yeah, try me now!" My lion roar was just filling me up
and the schoolyard, too.

There is *nuthin* wrong with the knowledge of some choice swear
words that you can use for your protection when you do need to roar.
That said, it's easy to fall into the habit of cussing unnecessarily. In
elementary school, I still needed the wisdom of restraint as to when
and where cussing was advisable. As a rapper, ain't gonna lie, I didn't
shy away from drippin' when it rhymed. Once I started doing comedy
videos and then stand-up, I got wisdom. Comedy works without cusswords and I didn't need profanity if I wanted to appeal to a broader

audience. In fact, I think when comics swear too much, it can become a crutch.

Back in Millen as a little kid, however, it *sho'nuff* felt good to get those bullies off my back. From then on, I could be myself—funny, a free spirit—but nobody was gonna make me afraid. Nobody. No matter how unfair the world was, I was not going to lose my positivity or my exuberance. Only one fear got to me at times—my concern that the curse of addiction might be in my blood and that I would have to fight it like the Devil when the time came.

Wisdom Begins with Inspiration

We all think we know what success is gonna look like and feel like until we get there and realize, *Aw, shucks, this ain't all that.* Sometimes, you can gain knowledge of your possibilities when you see somebody else's success. Finding the wisdom as to *how* to achieve those possibilities really begins with inspiration.

At the age of eight, I saw an inspiring vision of success when I made friends with players on the baseball team who were white and who lived like people did on TV. One of my white teammates, especially, became a good friend. He had a momma and a daddy living under the same roof of a house that they owned. When I visited him the first time, I was greeted by his parents, who were attached at the hip. They welcomed me in unison, waving me into the kitchen.

"Glad you could come over to our house!" his momma said. "Our humble home," his daddy added. It was a three-bedroom ranch-style house, nothing extra. But I was wide-eyed. To me, it was a mansion.

The refrigerator was overflowing with fresh food and healthy beverages, like a mini grocery store. And cheese sticks!

Out front, the family's four-wheeler had a spot for everybody's personalized fishing pole. Even the little baby daughter had her own pink fishing pole over there. Mind-boggling. She wasn't even catching fish! She was maybe just playing with gummy worms, pretending they could be bait.

It gave me something to dream that I could have one day and that was good knowledge to have. Believing that it was possible was one thing, but knowing *how* to get that money was a whole other thing.

I didn't know exactly *how* 2Pac had done it, except that he was like an overnight superstar—barely out of high school and, next thing, he's selling millions of albums and acting in big movies. He created the Outlawz—who were like his posse but did their own thing, too. I liked that he took the people he loved along on his ride. Even though I was only eight-and-a-half, I started counting the years it would take for me to follow 2Pac's footsteps.

Then, one day, around the start of the school year, I got the shock of my life after getting on the bus that my sisters and I rode to and from school every day. I'd just taken my seat up at the front of the bus when one of the older girls came over and asked, "You hear about 2Pac?"

"No, what?"

Other kids leaned in.

The girl-in-the-know said, "Pac died." Nobody seemed to react.

"Aw, hell no!" I argued. "Who said that? They made that up."

She insisted, "No, he got shot couple days ago in Las Vegas."

Pac could not die. He had been shot before. He always came back. It was a lie.

"Don't you call me a liar!" This girl insisted she saw the article in the newspaper. Pac was dead.

With tears starting to run down my face, I hung my head and rushed to the back of the bus, where I cried like a baby. For the next two days I felt crushed, like my dreams had been shot down, too.

This was my equivalent to being forced out of the Garden of Eden. In punishment for eating the fruit of the Tree of Knowledge of Good and Evil, Adam and Eve became mortal and had to work the land by the sweat of their brow. 2Pac had seemed larger-than-life and he had more knowledge than most teachers and preachers. You could hear it in his words. He seemed to know everything about everything. And yet, Pac had moved so fast into his fame that he had not gone through enough to gain the wisdom to put his knowledge to use—possibly as to how to avoid the beefs or the wrong influences that maybe got him killed.

My strategy for moving past the loss was to try to remember the three-day rule. When Jesus was crucified, he told his followers not to seek vengeance and not to mourn past three days, because he would no longer be where his body had been left, that he would have risen by then.

I tried to find some wisdom for myself after the murders of 2Pac in September 1996 and Biggie in March 1997. Maybe that was why I made an early decision to avoid guns altogether. Maybe that was also why I started to freestyle words that were less about killing and more about ladies.

After 2Pac died, I grew up even more and decided not to waste a minute of the time that had been given to me. It was also around this stage of life that I started to be more careful about who I could trust or not trust. Knowledge told me that, when push comes to shove, human beings can commit wrongs and make mistakes. We have weaknesses, temptations, and we can come under negative influences. In other words, be careful with your trust and use your knowledge of human nature when you choose who you let into your inner circle.

When it comes to the question of trust, wisdom helps align you with your Higher Power's guidance. So, I've found, in making any important decisions, the best answers come from combining your own knowledge of human nature and worldly situations with the wisdom that comes from always trusting God's guidance.

Name Your Lessons

You might just be surprised when you start paying more attention to the difference between knowledge and wisdom in your life. When you feel alone and unsure about the road ahead, try connecting to the voice of the sunflower that lives in you.

Don't be embarrassed to be curious or to ask questions when you go in search of important answers. The more you know, the deeper you go, the more knowledge and wisdom you will turn up. When you identify a lesson that has helped you, name it and claim it. Is it knowledge you can use in the future? Does it offer you wisdom for growth?

Just like the Bible says, "*Seek, and ye shall find.*" The next challenge, after you've gained knowledge and the wisdom to put it to use, is to share it with somebody else who needs it more.

Check out the people you know and whether they have knowledge and/or wisdom. The differences usually show up quickly.

Buddy, the sugar daddy, has worldly knowledge about how to get women into bed. But not a lot of wisdom. After all, as he keeps having to learn, "You don't want to get every lovely ladeeee into bed unless you care to wake up with bed bugs."

Drip has a lot of wisdom from the streets. He's wise enough to know that you should never judge a book by its cover. As Drip tells the girls who don't think he's too smart, "Yuh, don't judge me by the way I talk. Look at how I walk." Drip doesn't always know how to get the knowledge he needs. He doesn't know that when his probation officer tells him he's not allowed to leave the City and he shows up on a New York TV show to promote his album that he may have to go spend a month in jail. Then again, after Drip made it onto national media, his music career skyrocketed.

He definitely gained some wisdom from all that.

CHAPTER 4

WHEN THE WORST HAPPENS

Stay Up!

I f I had to pick the *least*-appreciated lesson that can give you the most mileage in every situation, it is the importance of *staying up*.

When my road to success as a rapper ran into challenges, this lesson helped me come up with a different plan. Whenever my kids need me to be there for them with advice, comfort, and support, this is also the first guidance I always give to them, no matter how young they are. When the whole comedy club world shut down due to the pandemic and I was at a monthly overhead of $75,000—which is mouths to feed and shoes to put on feet—I started over from scratch by putting this powerful tool to use.

Anytime you are broke and hurting, you gotta find your footing and stay up, hard as that may be. It may be as simple as telling yourself there is something that you are supposed to learn from whatever it is you are going through. When you learn how to do it, you can turn your life around so fast you'll get whiplash—in a good way. Whenever you are setting out on a new venture, experience, or move, staying up will keep you from being thrown off by little things that go wrong.

What about when big things go wrong? Those are the times when it's more important than ever to teach yourself to stay up. And the same goes for when the very worst happens—something I had to learn much too early.

The Curse of Addiction

The first time I realized that Momma and Pops had started doing a little coke now and then was in the spring of 1998. I was ten-and-a-half years old and finishing up the fourth grade. Pops would come by on occasion and snort a line or two with Momma or leave her a little of her own to use. Not much.

We'd been living in the single-wide tin-can trailer owned by my grandmomma Mary for a few years and my sisters, teenagers already, didn't want me to share their bedroom anymore. That meant I slept on the sofa bed in the living room—and could see what was going on in the kitchen. By this point, I knew Momma would drink and smoke weed but that was it. That was until one night after Pops had dropped over briefly. I could see Momma sitting at the kitchen table with some of her homegirls laying out a line of white powder on something like a popsicle stick to sniff it up real fast. The men—the boyfriends of the homegirls—who I could see through the sliding glass door, were outside snorting something, too. After everyone left, Momma cleaned up the kitchen, humming softly, and sat down again to sniff up another line of the powder. Everything was quiet and I drifted off to sleep.

The next morning, a Saturday, Momma was up dusting the fake fireplace and I directly asked her, "Momma, how come you put that white powder up your nose?"

She answered with an embarrassed look on her face. "'Cause it make me feel good, son."

My first reaction was that she deserved to feel good. But then I had a bad feeling, maybe connected to my understanding of the curse of addiction. I never said to her that I wished she would stop and I never expressed any judgment. Some of our family members judged everyone and I wasn't going to do that. Still, I wished Momma could feel good without needing her escapes.

Whenever Pops stopped over and they did a little, I had mixed feelings. On the one hand, I was suspicious of anything that made you feel so good you'd wanna do more and more. On the other hand, I also liked my father coming around. And sometimes he'd leave Momma some money, which I could tell because the fridge was better-stocked the next day.

There was still an attraction between Skip and Melissa—maybe more from him for her. But he had his charisma, too, and he could stay up, his way, and it would usually result in comedy. That was part of his appeal and why he was good as a boss. But I have to say that some of my daddy's swag was bought—because he was the Man in the Town, and at that time he had money and folks around who were impressed by him. But my momma had something else—a glow that warmed everyone around her. She knew how to shift the energy in the room and make you feel good—a key to staying up as an art form.

Momma was the original Real One. Her swag was almost too much. With an education, opportunity, someone to encourage and open a few doors for her, she could have been a star. Or, with the right circumstances, she could have used her sense of style to go into fashion design or started a business of her own.

There were only two times I can remember when I saw Momma really break down. The first instance was around the same time period when Grandmomma Mary gave Momma an older Cutlass in need of lots of work. Momma put all her government check money into fixing it up real nice to drive us to school and be able to go to the store and everything.

Well, when my uncle, Momma's brother Chris, sees it, he says he wants it, and goes back to Grandmomma Mary and says, "Momma, I need that Cutlass more than Melissa!" His argument is that we live in the trailer that belongs to Grandmomma Mary, so by rights he deserves the car, even though Momma spent all her money fixing it up.

Next thing I know, Momma's bust out crying on the phone, begging her mother, "You know I fixed up the car for me and my kids. I done put all my government checks in this car."

There was *nuthin* Momma could say to get her brother and my grandmother to change their minds. They suggested, "Tell Skip to get you a car."

"That ain't fair," was all I could say. Momma was trusting and kind to a fault. A lot of the family took advantage of that and it used to make me so mad.

Momma said, "Aw, let it go." Pops was in a position to buy Momma a car. But he chose not to. So that meant my mother had to get a favor from one of the sugar daddies who called on her for favors. I got even more mad about that. But, *dang*, if one of those old men didn't own some used car lot and if she didn't go get us a raggedy ancient Honda. Who cared? It was a car of our own. Momma raised up her own spirits and drove the three of us kids to our different schools every morning in that old beat-up car like it was a Cadillac.

Another time I saw Momma really break down was when my grandmomma Mary moved to Florida—at a time when we really could have used the help. My grandmomma was with her husband then, Mr. John. He was disabled, in a wheelchair, and insisted that they move to Fort Lauderdale for an easier life for him. Momma took it hard. They hadn't been gone long when I heard her sobbing on the phone with her momma, saying, "Momma, I need you. I can't live without you." She begged my grandmomma to come back.

Grandmomma Mary was so stubborn. She wasn't about to move back to Millen because her daughter was struggling.

Momma hung up the phone and laid her head in her hands. I offered, "I could just stay home from school and spend the day with you, what you think?" hoping that would cheer her up.

"Only person who stays home is gonna clean my house!" Momma said, wiping her tears away. She was serious, too.

By later that evening, Momma was in a better mood. Her moment of weakness had passed and—*bam*—she had her swag and spirit back all the way.

Momma was so real that she had a habit of saying the things *out loud* that most people only think. The example that stays with me to this day is this unexpected thing she said to me one night while I was in the bathtub. In the tin trailer there was no such thing as privacy.

Momma walked in, a lit blunt in her hand, and, without looking directly at me, said, kinda to herself, "You better have a big dick."

Huhhhh?

It wasn't mean or demanding, more like she had prayed for that for me and was thinking about how somebody coming out the mud had to find ways to be confident and walk cocky-like into any situation. She could have said "You better be tall," or "You better be the star I think you are." Either way, makes sense that you'd wanna walk with that air of command, as if you did have a big one between your legs. "Like your daddy," she added.

As much as I knew about almost *everything* around then, I had no clue that this was anything more than something the rappers would boast about. In fact, my first thought—I was ten-and-a-half years old—was to ask myself, almost joking, *She talkin' about my wee-wee?*

A couple of years later when they taught sex education at school, there were giggles and comments about size and I figured it out more. Well, sort of. In school, Georgia law said that everything we learned about sex education had to be about abstinence only. I couldn't even pronounce it (still can't) let alone learn how to actually abstain.

Momma may have meant her comment literally. I've heard other mothers express their hopes that their sons would grow up "well-endowed." But, on another level, I think my mother just wanted me to shine and, being real, she wanted her kids to be blessed.

Melissa Coney didn't have the means to give us everything she wanted for us. Instead, she focused on praying those things into existence. And that's how she stayed up—even when harsh things happened. Every now and then, she would also send a message to us just so we'd remember what was important—like the words she wrote right under my picture in my fourth-grade yearbook.

I remember vividly how she sat down at the kitchen table and looked over everything my friends and teachers had written to me in it. I could see by her smile that she was pleased. My grades were good. I was popular, doing great in sports, and even recognized for my talents at freestylin. Momma was so proud, she read over all the messages, every single one.

Then I watched as she reached for a pen, thought for a minute, and began to look for where to sign my yearbook, too. Momma wrote right under my picture: "To my best friend Dewayne, Stay smart!"

To this day, whenever I need help staying up, I think back to her message and it raises my spirit on the spot.

Momma was clearly giving me her grade-A seal of approval. It made me so proud that she saw me as her best friend, and that she was always going to be my biggest fan. In hindsight, I think, by her words, she also wanted me to stay drug-free and to outsmart the curse.

For the rest of that summer—which we spent in Atlanta—and into the early fall back in Millen, I mostly wasn't worrying about no curse of addiction. Momma was in good spirits. She was healthy and talking about finding us a better place to live, even surprising us with new sneakers she'd found on sale at the Dollar General Store. Blue-suede Adidas.

"Dewayne," the girls at school tried to tease me, "you wearin' women sneakers!"

Really? I glanced down at my feet. They looked fly to me.

"Those are so two years ago! And they fake," somebody else added mockingly. I guess they had one too many stripes on them.

All I did was smile with embarrassment and quietly mention that's what made them classic. I was learning at that time not to care what anyone else said or thought. But when I got home, I couldn't help asking Momma, "Why would you send me to school in fake women's Adidas?"

"Because they look good. Don't matter how much they cost. It's how they make you feel."

"Well, I feel cheap."

Looking back, I realize that she was trying to make me happy within her budget and I was being ungrateful. My uncles and even my daddy came over to try to convince me my fake blue-suede Adidas were fine. My daddy drove up in a new Mustang with a pocket full of money and wearing some brand-new Nike Air Max.

Inside, I was in disbelief. It would have been easy for my pops and uncles to have offered to buy me some better shoes. When I saw that they didn't offer, I knew that I had to get up fast to make my momma feel better—because they weren't gonna do it.

That's when I knew it was my job to stay up because my momma needed that.

I shifted fast from ungrateful to grateful. Those shoes didn't make me. I still was me. And I was not going to let anything bring me down.

Besides that, I could feel brighter days ahead. Momma was reading her Bible more often than in the past. We were even going to church now and then on Sundays.

Everything was cool. Until it wasn't.

Undone

Some people say that good news comes fast. In my experience, bad news, when you least expect it, comes even faster.

The date when things started to come undone in our tin-can trailer was December 8, 1998, the day before my eleventh birthday. That was when Momma must have gotten some cocaine from someone other than my daddy.

The story I heard down the road was that Pops came through that night and he tried some of what she had snorted earlier.

He said to her, "Somethin's not right with this cut. Don't smell right. It's bad, Melissa. Lemme give you some of mine."

Momma apparently complained that she thought something was wrong with it, too, because her head was hurting. After that, though, I think she did a couple of lines with my Daddy and started to feel better. But later in the night she started feeling *real* sick. Her head was worse, and she called Auntie Ruby and said, "I need to go to the hospital."

All of that I pieced together later on. The best I can remember is that when Ruby brought Momma home from the Millen hospital, I was waiting up, feeling uneasy. Right at this point, everything becomes clear in my memory. First, Momma comes in wearing a neck brace. She looks at me, right in the eye, asking for something but not saying *nuthin.*

"What, Momma? What the hospital say?"

"They say I got a pinched nerve in my neck," Momma says slowly, holding the wall to steady herself. In a sudden move, she then snatches the neck brace off and tells me, "It ain't my neck, it's my head." The pain is so bad she can hardly talk. I reassure her and help her into bed.

The next morning, Momma sleeps in and I start to think she's come down with a flu maybe. The next two days go by and she stays in the bed. On Friday, she's coming out of the bathroom and we hear her call, "Torrie, Shavonne, and Dewayne, get up. Y'all need to go to school!"

We go running and she's sitting down in the hallway. Momma just nods, and tells my sister, "Torrie. Call 911. I need an ambulance." This means that they'll take her to a better hospital, over in Augusta—about an hour's drive north of Millen.

Torrie, trying not to be too worried, announces that the ambulance should be here any minute and then, keeping things normal, asks, "Well, I guess this means I can't go to a friend's house today?" Momma comes back with her usual, "As long as my house is clean, you can go on over there."

We all start to relax. And when the ambulance arrives, the driver, who knows Momma and probably saw her earlier in the week at the store, I guess, comes into the trailer and asks if she can walk outside or if he needs to get her up onto a gurney.

Momma's weakly trying to stand to even see if she can walk.

"Melissa," he scolds her, "why you doin' this?" I watch as he takes her by each shoulder and shakes her. "You know ain't *nuthin* wrong with you."

For a quick instant, I see my mother's hands and arms spasm, then droop at her side like a rag doll's. But then she's talkin' again, so I tell myself to be positive, pray, and know she'll be fine.

I walk out with the driver and Momma on the gurney, and as we go I'm telling her to rest. She's weak, in a lot of pain, but conscious enough to wave and nod when I say that I'll see her soon. Out of a sense of duty, we call Grandmomma Mary, who decides she best get in the car with Mr. John and drive the eight hours up from Fort Lauderdale to the hospital in Augusta. Over the weekend I go visit Momma in the hospital but we don't get to talk. Everyone says she's resting and in good hands so I go home and wait until Monday, December 14, for further updates.

The only information about Momma that came to me over the weekend was that it began as a bleed in her brain, like a burst blood vessel. Secondary to that she had a stroke, diagnosed at the hospital. Nobody said that she was not out of the woods yet or that she might take a turn for the worst. I had no reason to think anything other than the best. I had just turned eleven and, looking back over my whole life, I couldn't remember my mother being sick. My grandmomma Mary assured me that Melissa was tough, always, and would be coming home before long.

So, on Monday night, I was at the home of my dad's girlfriend Wilhelmina where I was staying while Momma was in the hospital, waiting for word. As soon as Pops got home, he walked into the room and first thing I asked was, "Pops, you heard anything about Momma today from Mr. John?" We all liked Mr. John and he was the one relaying medical updates about Momma to everyone.

"Yeah, I talked to Mr. John . . ."

"What he say?"

"He say . . . Uh, he . . ." My daddy was holding something in and then couldn't anymore. In disbelief he said, "She didn't make it, son." He bust out crying, something I'd never seen.

I fell out crying and crying—with not just disbelief but shock and anger and devastation. It was not only the worst thing that had ever happened, but on top of the loss, it came with no signs, no reason to even fear we could ever lose her.

My heart was broken. Maybe permanently. Maybe the heartbreak of losing my mother at that young age made it so no one or *nuthin* could break my heart in the future.

Every what-if in the universe pounded inside my brain. What if I had done more to protect her? What if we had not lived with so much stress? Some people might say drugs killed her or the curse did her in. But I would forever believe it was poverty—which, from then on, became my mortal enemy.

Nothing made any sense, except for a passing thought that came to me. Plain and simple, I was *not* going to allow the worst that had happened beat me down in the eyes of others. I was *not* going to be that poor, pitiful Kountry boy whose momma died, only to be forgotten. I was going to make her live through me. I was going to live my life as if she was watching over me every minute of every day and I would know, too, how proud she was of me.

My life was *not* going to be made smaller for Momma being gone. No, it was going to be the opposite. My life was going to be richer and greater for her having been my mother.

This was my conviction: If the worst could happen so, too, the best could happen. Being positive and finding a way to *stay up* took on a new meaning. And from the day of Momma's death forward, I was determined never to be in a position where I had to ask a family member or anyone for anything. Staying up was also my way of letting Momma know in heaven that she had raised me to be great.

Not very long ago (actually, during the first wave of the pandemic), I found out that nobody had paid Momma's funeral charges. I apologized and made the payments that same day, as my momma would have had me do. I couldn't believe that bill had gone unpaid for over twenty years. After Momma died and arrangements were being made, apparently certain family members had come around telling the lady at the funeral parlor, "Y'all better fix her hair right!" I never wanted to see Momma in a casket, which probably explains why I took my time getting to the viewing. Everybody else had gone but the lady in charge waved me on in, telling me, "You can go up and see her, son." It was dark and sinister in there, like a scary movie. The lady turned one light on, but I couldn't do it.

"Naw," I said, but thanked her just the same. Momma was somewhere else. I'd cried enough.

In the six months that followed, my sisters stayed in the trailer with our grandmomma and Mr. John, and I went to live with my daddy for the first time in my life. He couldn't understand why nothing ever made me very upset. If he was on me to do something or disciplining me for some misbehavior, I'd never get down. It wasn't worth it.

Even though I spent the next six years bouncing around and staying with different relatives, for all intents and purposes, at age eleven I took charge of myself and made it my business to see that my sisters were protected and had the help they needed, too.

When the worst happens, a lot of times it means you man up or woman up *fast*. The key is finding your own motivation for how to *stay up*.

At Momma's funeral, I allowed myself to cry. Not too much, though. Everyone else made up for the tears I held back. Grandmomma Mary was the one crying the hardest and the loudest. But where was she when her daughter, the kindest person in the world, had asked her momma to come back from Florida, when she was needed most? The whole time my grandmomma bawled her eyes out, I thought, *Where had she been when Momma put her government check money into the car that my grandmomma decided my uncle could scoop up after it was fixed?*

My stomach tightened to hear all of them praise Momma to the skies with words they'd never said to her face. My heart hurt to see my sisters mourning every day in the weeks and months that followed, and really for years. But I knew it wasn't going to serve me to mourn forever or to be mad. My plan was to give Momma her due in this life and to make the name of Melissa Coney resound in heaven.

At Momma's funeral, for a passing moment I imagined how everyone who had ever refused to help my mother would one day have to come to me in need and have to eat from my hand. I let that anger go, but the vision stayed with me: out of all my daddy's children, it would be me, Melissa's son, who would rise above the rest, and everyone would have to give the credit and the praise to her.

Look for Something Positive
You Can Do with Your Pain

The proven path for learning how to *stay up*—especially when the worst happens—will never be the same for each of us. But I will say that too much of the time we all tend to focus on what's wrong instead of appreciating the things that are right.

My solution to that is Kountry simple. Think of the lessons you've already learned from your worst times or even from your good times. Have you ever had to get past your own sadness to make someone else feel less sad? Give yourself some praise and collect those good deeds you've done. They should make you feel good.

There is a saying that time heals all wounds. But that misses the point. Instead of trying to forget the hurt, it's more powerful to look for something positive you can do with your pain. Instead of drowning your sadness in liquor or dulling your senses, maybe you can choose to feed yourself with something good to read or to get on down with people you love who could use your company. And vice versa. You can practice the art of staying up by making a list of things that raise your spirit.

When Drip faces a situation that could bring him down, he'll land on an idea so he can reinvent himself and stay up. After a series of headaches and some moments of not being able to see well, he realized he needed glasses and went off to a jeweler to get Cartier frames with diamonds on them. When he tried them on, it was the new him. More intelligent and sophisticated. "Yuh, ready to read words I don't even know!"

When Buddy gets down—like if one of his girls gets herself a real boyfriend—he moves on and focuses on meeting other girls. That's how to stay up like a sugar daddy. Buddy's big pickup line is, "Dahlin', put your number in my phone and don't be stressed . . . if you wanna get blessed." He has a whole list of lines like that one.

Stand-up comics are supposed to have a notepad near their bed at night or in their pocket to write down ideas that cross their minds for a funny line or bit. That's called inspiration. When you come up with a joke out of thin air, that's a gift from God. One of my favorite moments of *Seinfeld* is from an episode where Jerry scribbles down an idea for a joke in the middle of the night but then can't read his writing later on. Hilarious.

Some people seem surprised when I say Jerry Seinfeld is one of my big comedy influences, but he's an OG for real—first, as a stand-up comic; second, as a content creator who translated his style of observational humor for TV, pitching *Seinfeld* as "a show about nothing." What's really gangsta is how the series has also generated almost $4 billion in revenues, making it the number one, most-profitable sitcom in the history of Hollywood. Jerry is smart, a brilliant businessman/ producer. And everyone in his cast has benefited from his success. I have taken a lot of inspiration from Seinfeld when coming up with relatable yet off-the-wall concepts for my videos.

Rather than jotting down ideas, I've gotten in the habit of texting someone on my team to make sure I don't forget or have my own trouble reading my writing.

Again, you don't have to be a stand-up to jot down ideas for how to stay up. Maybe you want to come up with business ideas for a side hustle or to remember where you were when you saw something that took your breath away. Keep those memories close for when the worst things happen and let them stay for times when you most need them to soothe and lift your soul.

CHAPTER 5

THE BIRTH OF KOUNTRY WAYNE

Your Rep Is Everything

G rowing up, I heard friends say, *"Your rep is everything,"* but I didn't get it. What I missed and didn't fully appreciate until my career took off is that your reputation can start early in your life and it will follow you from then on. Your rep is not engraved in stone, but it's hard to reinvent your rep once things you actually or supposedly did or said get out into the world and too much time goes by. A bad rep can be harmful while a positive rep can be your magic charm to open doors that even money can't open.

Your rep can be your leverage. If you don't have leverage that can take you from one stage of the game to the next, you are vulnerable. But *with* leverage from a solid rep, people will treat you better and take you more seriously. Your rep can get you ahead without money, too. It can also be your Get Out of Jail Free card—every once in a while.

You are never too young or too old to start appreciating the fact that your rep is everything. With all my mistakes and missteps, I'm thankful that the details didn't follow me forever and that I've been able to repair my rep enough to enjoy just being who I am in public and in private. Y'all young'uns—and grown folk, too—these days you have to worry about incidents when you don't use your best judgment in what you say and do, only to see everything blasted out on social media for everyone to see. That's hard enough in real time, but what's even worse is down the road when the same marks against you turn up, say, if you apply for a job or a bank loan. Social media was how I built a fan base, so I appreciate its potential. The flip side is that the minute you or somebody else takes out their phone, your rep is instantly on the line. The watchwords are *proceed with caution whenever you go online.*

When in doubt, the best way to protect your rep is just to be the best version of yourself. And if you fall from that standard, try to change your ways. As I say to my kids, in some instances, "Do as I say and not as I did."

The Man in the Town

It was in Atlanta that I first learned the importance of having a rep, but it was in Millen, starting in the fifth grade, where I really began to earn one. This was not long after Momma died—and by now Pops had decided that I should change my last name to Colley. Most people knew I was his son but now that I had his last name, I was like Simba in *The Lion King*—the firstborn son expected to eventually take over as the Man in the City. Or, to be more accurate at the time, as the Man in the Town. Most people also knew that I was Melissa Coney's son, and the talk soon became that I had inherited her charisma and good looks.

The embarrassment of never having money was also suddenly lifted. That was from Momma. Her blessings from heaven began almost immediately after she died. It turned out the little bit she had put into Social Security gave us death benefits that amounted to $200, per month, for each of her three children. For the first time in our lives, my sisters and I could buy ourselves new clothes and shoes—not from the Dollar General Store or Goodwill but from stores like the Gap and Footlocker. Momma had taught us style and now we could afford to treat ourselves. We knew how to budget, *fo sho,* but for me this money from my momma was a chance to wash off some of the poverty that had been on us for so long.

This was only a taste. But I felt rich already and I couldn't wait to make more money. By this age, I was starting to have an idea how my daddy and uncles made a living and I pretty much assumed that, when the day came, I'd go into the family business. Hustle was in my genes, after all, and, being real, I could see myself as a playa and a boss like my daddy Skip, but with smarts, good looks, and swagger like Melissa Coney. That was my formula for popularity—and an equation for one day getting out of Millen and achieving fame and fortune.

The blessing of that monthly check went beyond having nice things I never had. In Atlanta, during my summer stays with Aunt Betty, I still had my Kountry rep, but I had enough City style to be taken more seriously when I let it be known that rap was in my future. These were the early days of Atlanta-based hip-hop getting credibility and starting to take over Southern hip-hop. By the time I was in middle school, local rappers like Ludacris and the duo of Outkast were getting national fame, putting Atlanta on the map. In truth, I loved the flavor of R & B—Usher was Atlanta's crown prince by then—but the problem was I couldn't sing worth a damn. So rapping was my calling card.

Atlanta had its own style—like Kris Kross made famous—and even a dance scene called the Bankhead Bounce, and another hip-hop dance trend was called "ticking." It was all relevant to me—from the streets and from real experience.

I wasn't gonna rap about hustling in those years. But I was writing lyrics all the time about getting girls. My popularity gave me the confidence to talk about how good it was gonna be for her to feel my "chocolate touches," taste my "chocolate kisses," and enjoy my "red velvet cake hands and vanilla ice cream words." Clearly, I had a sweet tooth.

Meanwhile, back in Millen, in middle school, I'd entertain my friends with my raps but *nuthin* drew a bigger crowd on our breaks from school than stories about the men in my family and their way with women.

Sometimes I'd just imitate my dad or my Coney uncles, Cleave and Beave, and act like I was experienced.

My boys would give me a hard time, sayin' stuff like, "Wayne, you never had no sex!"

"Well, when I do, I'll know what to do!" That made sense, so they'd listen up.

"Like what?"

"You gotta get a woman in the mood."

"How?"

I was a little unclear on the specifics of foreplay, but I quoted Pops and said, "You got to get the grease hot before you put the chicken in."

Everyone would laugh—except for a few, who were confused.

"If it ain't wet, it ain't ready yet." I was repeating what my uncle Cleave would say. But I really had no idea how to actually do the deed.

My uncle Beave had the best advice for making sure that the

woman was having as much fun as the man. It was his job to make sure, too. Beave's words of wisdom, which I passed on, were "If she don't moan, it ain't grown."

Mannnnnn, everyone would stand there, dazzled. I'd serve up tasty Kountry morsels like that all day long. At the least, I was performing a public service announcement—because they taught us *nuthin* in sex ed.

For the six months or so that I was with Pops, I not only got to know him, his better and his worse, but I also got to know my closest Colley brother—Arby. All my brothers stayed with their own mommas. My brothers each had their own personalities and reputations, but generally, none of them would say they had to grow up as fast as me. So even when I was in the fifth and sixth grades, they sort of deferred to me for my opinions and advice.

My time living under the same roof as Pops first started at Miss Wilhelmina's house. She was kind and stable, didn't do drugs, and knew her way around the kitchen. *Mannnnnn,* she made the best spaghetti and meatballs I ever ate, before or after. With my daddy's weakness for women, I predicted his eye would roam eventually. And it only took him two months before he moved out to be with a new girlfriend. She was easygoing and good-looking, but she and my father were both under the influence on a regular basis. They kind of let me come and go as I wanted—which I liked. On the other hand, they'd forget mealtimes and groceries and all that. So they'd send me to Dairy Queen. Eventually, that got old so I'd sneak over to Miss Wilhelmina's for spaghetti or whatever she was serving up. By the time summer rolled around, I was ready for the City.

My first thought was, *At last, I'm gonna get some structure.* My next thought was that I had to make sure my monthly payment was forwarded to an adult in Atlanta—otherwise, I wouldn't have that money.

We worked it all out and off I went. When I returned that fall, Pops had disappeared. Out of my life, more or less, all over again.

How was I supposed to feel? My heart was still heavy from losing Momma. Now I didn't know where my daddy was. It was all a reminder of the curse of addiction—my one fear. Deep down, I knew that if something terrible had happened to Pops, somebody would've told me. Instead, everyone just acted like that was Vincent Colley—part of his rep as a hustler, playa, and outlaw—and that he'd turn up soon.

Naturally, I was disappointed, but the feeling was like just another weight I had to carry and not let it get to me, even if it was as heavy as cement. Over time, I found a way for the feeling to lessen and to know he had his curse to figure out. Whatever was going on, it was his battle. Not mine. Still, it was a letdown that, after all those years of my daddy being absent from my life, he'd come back for a minute, then left again. The idea of having a family of my own was more and more appealing, not because I was ready but because I couldn't wait to prove that it was possible to be consistent as a father.

My rep was not gonna be based on refusing to forgive—because that hardens your heart.

The only people I would really hold accountable were my momma and daddy because they were parents and supposed to be consistent. In the future, I would look to my daddy for information about things he knew that I didn't—although I was careful about trusting anyone other than myself.

Once I realized Pops wasn't gonna be around for awhile, I moved back into the tin-can trailer with Grandmomma Mary, Mr. John, and my sisters. After Momma died, my grandmomma wanted to go back to Florida but Shavonne refused to leave her friends and school. I was proud of my sis for standing up for herself but in the long run we really needed to be out of the small town. Grandmomma Mary and Mr. John agreed to stay in Millen from then on. For the next couple of years, we all did our best to avoid the crowding but I was always relieved when summer rolled around and it was time to go to Atlanta with Auntie Betty and my cousins.

By my early teens, it wasn't much of a culture shock or an adjustment. My Kountry rep switched up easily to being in the City. By the end of the summer, I'd talk faster and act a little slicker and get back in time to impress everyone with tales of the Atlanta streets. The only problem adjusting again to Millen was living with my grandmomma. I felt like a man already, but I was living under her roof. I'd also ask questions that were uncomfortable for Grandmomma, who legally received our Social Security checks. She was offended if I asked about how much she was getting and how much she was actually spending on us.

Then Grandmomma put Mr. John out and got a new man, who we called Mr. Sidney.

"Did she really get rid of a man in a wheelchair for a man who had legs?" I asked my sisters.

Mr. Sidney was unpleasant for a most peculiar reason—*bad breath!* It was so bad we could not be in the same room with him if he so much as tried to open his mouth.

"Grandmomma put out a man who couldn't walk for a man who shouldn't talk," was my assessment.

Torrie, Shavonne, and I would make excuses to run outside if we were caught in the same space and forced to smell that breath. I don't know how Grandmomma Mary managed to ignore that sickening odor. (She must have lost her sense of taste and smell years before Covid.)

There came a time when Grandmomma decided she was done with my remarks, and especially my questions about where our money was going. One day I came home from school and outside the front door of the trailer was a garbage bag filled with my stuff. My Social Security check was taped to the bag, along with a letter that said, "You are no longer welcome to stay in my house."

The two people I called next were Jackie, my cousin on my daddy's side, and her mother, Momma Doog. And it was incredible how fast they arrived to pick me up. It was like my momma had been talking to them and they were waiting for the call.

Jackie and Momma Doog celebrated my arrival at their home like I was the Second Coming. They bought me even more clothes and shoes and pampered me to no end. In the summertime I continued to go to Atlanta to give them a break and it was there that I was messing around one day in my cousin Travis's homemade recording studio in his basement and I started to use Kountry Wayne as my callout, with my claim-to-fame sign-off: "Swag right and everything."

Sounded so good. *It's ya boy, Kountry Wayne, swag right and everything.* It was like a bit of chocolate. You wanted more. I wasn't sure what that was. Not yet.

But could I really be a star, not just with a rep in Millen but in Atlanta, too?

I ain't gonna lie. One day I caught a glimpse of myself in the mirror. At thirteen, going on fourteen, I was, *sho'nuff, irresistible.*

Your Rep Starts Young

The rep I earned in eighth grade was a classic double-edged sword. The drama started because I was head over heels in lust with Latricia, who I'd been wanting to kiss since Head Start—we really did meet there. I was in full-on *teenage hormones* mode. She was, too.

We were too young to be trying to have sex, but in the midst of everything it seemed oddly natural. She followed me into the boys' bathroom one day after school and, it's like a movie that goes into slo-mo, I turn around to see her there, cute as can be, then we *go for it.*

We are both feeling good, so good that we don't hear the door open or see the janitor enter the boys' bathroom. Next thing we know, he starts yelling, "What y'all doin'?"

I pause for a minute and realize I really don't know.

So much for getting me some coochie!

Long story short, we didn't finish. And there was bad news and good news. The bad news was that I had to go to alternative school for the rest of the year—what they called the "jailhouse of the school" (which was crosstown by some railroad tracks and a cornmill). Alternative school was where they sent all the kids who get into trouble, the step before getting expelled. It wasn't even separated between eighth graders and twelfth graders. Like getting sent to prison for a parking ticket, if you are a first-time rule breaker, you come out a hardened criminal. The insult to injury was that I was having a good year in school and playing basketball, but I was kicked off the team for the rest of eighth grade. All bad news.

The good news, as far as I felt at the time, was that word spread overnight throughout the middle school and high school, which were connected on the same campus. My sister Torrie didn't think it was good news. She was so mad that even everyone in high school knew about what happened, and were coming up to her saying, "Heard your brother tearin' it up around here!" "Yo brother the man!" The story was the biggest thing to happen at school for weeks.

Torrie was embarrassed. Not me. Now I had a manly rep—even if it was based on only a partial truth. I was ready to go all the way—and soon!

Toward the end of the school year, a couple of new love interests came along. One of them was Tilquisha, who went by Queet. She was my age, super sweet, down-to-earth, straight-up Kountry, pretty (a future homecoming queen), and loving. We started to mess around but never got far enough for me to see what the fuss was really all about. A short time later, my other crush, Michelle, a year or so older than me, took me under her wing and showed me just what to do. *Mannnnnn,* I will be forever grateful to her—even if our teenage romance was short-lived.

I knew, from then on, that coochie was for me.

On that following Monday, I took off for Atlanta for the summer. Soon as I arrived, I was looking around the neighborhood for cute girls my age. In the blink of an eye, they are everywhere. I've got my swag right and everything. It's just a "What's up?" and a look that says, "Do you know what I know?"

Fourteen was the magic age for me. That summer I had so much sex, it became my fitness regimen. My upper body was still pretty lean and on the weak side, but all that hip action was a constant workout. From the waist down, I was supersonic.

The double-edged-sword part came later. Sure, I was on my way to becoming Kountry Wayne, swag right and everything, with a rep for having any girl I wanted. At fourteen! But, without intending it, I was getting hooked on coochie, not even paying attention to the grief I was trying to escape.

For all the years that I swore to avoid the curse of addiction to liquor or weed or drugs, I'd just substituted sex as my drug of choice.

Even if I didn't know it. On top of that, subconsciously it's possible I may also have been trying to create a family of my own to raise.

My male cousins in Atlanta were mad that the prettiest queen bees were buzzing for me. These were cousins who still thought of me as being Kountry, and they all made me out to be slow and not too smart. I shrugged and said, "Yeah, maybe, but have you looked at this face?"

My cousin argued that he was good-looking, too, but wasn't getting any girl action. My advice was, "You got to stay fresh." Girls love a man who takes pride in his appearance, after all. Then I told him what Uncle Cleave had said about taking your time. But mostly, after the Summer of Lust in Atlanta, I think my real secret was finding the right kind of female energy that connects for real with male energy. That's powerful. When you feel like she just needs some good lovin' and that you are not gonna hold it back, you are not just getting your lust unloaded, you are setting her wildness free.

But I still knew *nuthin* about the consequences of lust. When I got back to Millen for ninth grade, I made a beeline to go see Tilquisha. Our very next chance to be together was fireworks for both of us. From then on, I couldn't get enough of her, and vice versa. We must have gotten overly confident, thinking that we were being real careful, but I'm here to tell you, as I soon learned, the rhythm method is not an effective method of birth control. In the tenth grade, Queet came up pregnant a couple of times, which was sobering, although both of those instances ended up in miscarriage. We weren't trying to have kids, but we weren't trying too hard *not* to have them, either.

When poverty is your affliction, wrong choices lurk in all shadows. You only have to walk outside for something to grab you. Most of my homies from this period of my life got taken down from lack of wisdom, lack of options. Most became addicts young, got picked up for drugs, went to prison for guns, robbery, violence. All bad. In my mind, if I could make it past the age of twenty-two without using drugs, that was enough to beat the curse. At the same time, I wasn't really thinking about how much life would change or about how responsibilities would add up if I became a father too quickly. Nope, and I wasn't thinking about the consequences of unprotected teenage sex—which I should have been. I was too busy becoming the young Man in the Town.

Your Rep Gives You Value

Every now and then, I'd get a flash of the real world of Millen—in all its racist small-minded small-town glory. I don't believe a person is born racist. That said, racism *sho* does breed where there is poverty and ignorance together. And here is the problem: Racists don't even know they are racists. In rural Georgia, unless they are educated, white people will drop a slur on you as if it's a compliment. When I went to Jenkins High, white students were in the slight majority, say 60 percent, and the rest mostly Black and biracial. I was friends with everyone. That was part of my rep, too, and it was no secret that white girls flirted with me—and then some. But if a white girl and I ever started to get serious, she'd break it off, telling me her parents didn't approve.

"Because I'm Black?" I'd ask. That wouldn't get a straight answer. Soon they'd say things that would come down to the fact that I was Black and *poor*. "If you were Tiger Woods, no problem," they'd say. That seemed so hypocritical it made me wanna get out of Millen even faster.

All of this taught me a lot about not letting other people's judgments weigh in my spirit or harm the rep I'd earned already as having potential. I refused to let anyone else's bias limit my imagination.

I couldn't wait for my career as Kountry Wayne, rapper/star, to get underway for good. The fact that I was already known for being good with rhymes and performing made me take myself seriously—on top of having the confidence and charm needed to be a true entertainer. Rappers at this point were making all kinds of paper. So the way I felt, it was only a matter of time before that was gonna be my story. Then we'd see who was gonna date me or not. But I also knew potential was only of value up to a point. To really make it, I'd have to earn some bank to produce and promote the music the right way. My time in the City had taught me that. My plan then was to just enjoy my last two years of high school, maybe go to college near Atlanta, find a decent job in the music business, and use my reputation to build relationships.

By the age of twenty-three, I figured, I'd be on the radio. Those racist white parents would just have to see me rise and regret they didn't let their daughters date me.

But God had another plan. Right around Christmas in the eleventh grade, Queet let me know she was pregnant again. This time, no miscarriage followed. She was happy and I was scared. I told the important people in my family and got a mix of reactions. Some just saw me as grown already, so it was like they expected it all along. Grandmomma Mary—we were back on good terms by now—said, "Boy, I told you to leave them girls alone!" Momma Doog said, "Well, it's not about jes you anymore."

Then I went to talk to my daddy, who, by the way, was back in Millen after going missing for years and finally turning up in Brunswick, Georgia.

Pops was disappointed. He wanted me to be different from him and said, "You ruined your life." That was harsh. He added, "And you don't even know how to take care of yourself. How you gonna raise a baby?" When he said that, it instantly ignited my inner Michael Jordan to prove him wrong. I was gonna be the best dad in the world and having a baby was never gonna stop my flow.

High school fun, sports, messing around with whoever I so chose—all went out the window. As we approached the summer and Queet's due date in August, everything got a lot more serious. The most important consideration in my mind was coming up with a way to support my baby and my baby mama. My $200 monthly check wasn't going to be enough to cover formula, Pampers, and food for me and Queet, not to mention buy a car, car seat, stroller, playpen, and baby bed.

There wasn't anybody I knew who could give me the lowdown from a financial provider's point of view. So I sat down and did the math myself. If I got a job at one of the two plants left in town, I could make about $25,000 a year to start and go to community college nearby part-time. Then, I could graduate with a two-year degree and get a better job, improve my money, and that would let me save enough to get into music for real. Momma Doog and Jackie reassured me that even if it would take me longer, the college degree would be worth it.

After doing the research, I landed on the idea of getting a teaching degree and becoming a PE teacher. I was athletic, had played sports, mainly basketball, and was a good student, when I applied myself. Having a teaching degree worked out to approximately $30,000 a year and would keep me from having to lift heavy things in a factory job. After a couple of years teaching PE, I was confident that my career as a rapper would take over.

Ironically, the only teacher who resented my reputation and straight-up didn't like me was the technology teacher and basketball coach at our high school. The idea of becoming a great PE teacher gave me some strange satisfaction.

Unfortunately, the more I ran the numbers, the more I knew that the legit path for the next few years wasn't going to support a family and let me get my education. That's when I decided the most practical way forward was to hustle for a short time, on the weekends, only for a year or so. I'd get a legit job, too, support my family, go to college, and hustle and start a savings stash for my rap career. All I needed was enough money to get my foot in the door.

None of this was ideal. But I resolved to make it work.

Now that Pops was back in Millen, the thought did occur to me that an easier option was to get into hustling with him. I knew more by this point about who did what in my dad's operation, how the business was run, and how I could improve it. *Except*—he wasn't asking for my help.

When I went to talk to Pops about how to do my own thing and not step on his toes, I'll never forget the exchange we had with a woman we ran into as we walked along talking about specifics.

"Oh, hey, Vincent . . ." she began and then looked at me. To Pops, she continued, "This yo son?"

"This is Dewayne," Pops answered.

"Son of Melissa?" she asked. When my father nodded, the woman said, "Right, the smart one."

Pops said, "I thought he was the smart one. He got a baby on the way."

She gave me a disappointed look and walked away.

That look of hers cut deep. Maybe there was another way forward that didn't involve hustling. A fresh idea hit me: What if I enlisted? That would allow me to bring in a paycheck to take care of my family, pay for my education, and put aside money to get into music. I also felt a little proud imagining myself in uniform, leading an army unit and barking orders.

Pops was quick to jump onboard with the new plan. I think deep down he wanted me to keep my rep as the "smart one" and stay out of the drug game as long as possible. Because I was a minor, he went down to the recruiting office and signed for me to train with the Georgia National Guard. I would do Basic Training that summer before my senior year and then I'd go to Advanced Individual Training, which would prepare me for the Army National Guard after I graduated high school. AIT was designed to equip recruits with technical or trade skills that could be used in the service and beyond. The money I'd get would allow me to support my family, pay for college, and get rap going on the side.

Second thoughts soon set in. The closer I got to leaving for Basic Training, the more I dreaded it. But there was no turning back. We had a baby on the way and I wasn't going to cheat our son, Tony, out of the better life I knew was ours to give him.

My reputation might be hurt by other choices, but falling down on the job of being a daddy was not going to happen.

Does Your Rep Really Rep You?

Often, it's true that your reputation can precede you. That's not a terrible thing, as long as your rep actually represents you. If your rep is based on your track record of living your truth or staying up or any of the other principles that let you be the Real One on your own terms, that's a power you bring into the room the minute you walk in.

Now, if your reputation is fake or based on you trying to be someone you're not or on someone you used to be, you may have some explaining to do. If you've been a playa all your life and now you wanna turn over a new leaf, that's gonna take some time and effort.

Meanwhile, I recommend taking some time to consider how your reputation does or does not serve you. You might even want to ask other people you trust how they perceive your rep. Then you can decide if their impressions are fair or not. If not, you can choose to improve your rep by being the best you that you can be going forward. In the end, fortunately, people have short memories, after all, and with focus you can outgrow a bad rep.

How your rep works for you will depend on the world you want to conquer. On the streets, Drip lives up to his rep when he tells anyone, "Yuh, I'm the hottest in the Citeeee!" The streets agree. The loan officer at the bank feels differently, though, when Drip comes in with his sidekick T—to show him how it works in the corporate world—and tries to get a $25,000 loan. Drip comes in, offers his gold chain and diamond-encrusted teeth for collateral, and surprises the loan officer by kissing her. His rep on the streets does *not* work in her world. When Drip introduces T, the loan officer asks, "Oh, T is his name?" Drip responds, "Naw, that's his alias." "His alias?" Drip's unsure and answers, "His alien, I mean, yuh . . ." And it's all downhill from there.

Buddy lives up to his classic sugar daddy rep and has to constantly take out his rolls of money, his "presidents," to prove he has the goods. He loves to give girls more than what they asked for—one hundred, two hundred, and so on. But the real world always intrudes on Buddy's plans whenever he tries to get the girl to give him some collateral in exchange for his "investment" and he just returns to who he really is: "Yeahhhh, little dahlin'. Well, Buddy's just gonna take some of these presidents back."

My rep today as a comedian, entrepreneur, a dad with lots of kids, and a promoter of positivity, of course, is different from that of Buddy or Drip. But one thing we all have in common is a lust problem. No secret. There are all kinds of lust, by the way, not just what goes on between the sheets. Greed is a form of lust and so is envy. So is gluttony.

My rep at times is super different from the quieter lifestyle I enjoy after I'm done working. That's cool by me. So my rep works for me.

Don't be afraid to ask yourself if your reputation is working for you—or not. Don't be afraid to change up how you go about earning your rep. Do remember that striving to be the best you that you can be is not a bad way to reform a harmful rep. And if you don't know how, don't be afraid to ask someone who does.

CHAPTER 6

REAL WORLD

Be Passionate About *What* You Do, But Be More Passionate About *Who* You Do It For

One of the reasons I feel so confident in the principles and lessons I'm sharing with you is that I've had to learn and develop them for myself—through trial and *lots of error*. They are a proven commodity that have worked miraculously for me and are Kountry simple. Without them, I'd still be back in Millen, making the same mistakes and not knowing what I was doing wrong.

Another reason I believe in my own advice is that I've read many of the great self-help, prosperity, and business-success books out there on the shelves. Reading books can be the best food for thought! Everything you learn, especially when it comes from someone's real experience, is powerful. Actually, though, many of those books say the same thing. For example, almost everything I've heard or read about growth and success says that you should *be passionate about WHAT you do.*

You've probably read or heard that before, too. Makes sense, but that's not the whole story. I think you've got to go one step further and *be even more passionate about WHO you do it for.*

Passion is powerful. I don't care if you are pursuing money, love, opportunity, influence, knowledge, or wisdom. Passion is fuel. Passion drives you to be curious, ask questions, learn skills you need or that can help you advance toward achieving your goals. Passion is contagious. When you walk into a room to apply for a job or ask someone to invest in your idea, passion gets people to lean in. When an opportunity comes along and it could go to you or to someone else, passion can give you that extra drawing power.

But when you are passionate about who you are pursuing opportunities for, that raises the stakes. You walk into a room more than just excited to be there. You walk into a room with courage as well as purpose because you bring your commitment to the people who matter most to you.

When you are more passionate about the *who* than the *what,* you expand your playing field and remove the limitations on how far you can go.

This lesson, taught to me by my children, was once again learned the hard way. Parenthood is the most humbling experience in life. I didn't know that until the day came to pack up for Basic Training.

Facing Reality

"GET UP NOWWWWW! SOLDIERS, ATTENTION!" came the booming voice of a drill sergeant at 5:00 a.m. Or was this just a bad dream?

All that Kountry Wayne swag and young playa reputation I'd been flaunting vanished. Suddenly, I faced the reality that I didn't want to be in the Georgia National Guard or the US Army. Sure, I was fit and athletic, but it dawned on me that my strength was that of a young man, not a soldier.

The night before, we had traveled to the hottest, most humid, and dustiest backwoods spot in Oklahoma for Basic Training. I had been in the last bus, pulling up to the barracks at around four thirty in the morning.

This was a mistake and I knew it. For a half hour, I fell into a deep sleep, reminding myself, *You gotta do what you gotta do.* When the drill sergeant woke us up, I looked around bewildered, realizing that everyone was in the same situation.

We all scrambled from our bunks, jumping into formation in our gray short shorts and gray T-shirts with *Army* on the back, as the sergeant walked down the line in disgust, saying we were the most worthless-looking recruits he'd ever seen in his life.

I don't know what I expected. Of course, I knew we weren't gonna be eating ice cream and resting our tired legs all day. But nothing in my life had prepared me for hearing orders *barked* at us nonstop and being belittled for no reason. Nothing like this had ever come from even the more obnoxious Kountry coaches at Jenkins High.

Looking around at the mostly white big ole boys in my unit, I was thinkin', *Aw, hell no! What have I done?* I signed up for the Army, to serve my country, to make some money for my child about to be born, but I did not volunteer for *no sleep* and psychological warfare. From that moment on, I was determined to get the lowdown on how to get out of this torture.

Finally, I heard through the grapevine: "They let you go home, if you say you're thinking about committing suicide." Sounded good to me. It would take some acting on my part, but I'd spent years watching movies on the VCR. Not to mention I was good with my words. How hard could it be to convince a superior officer that you were feeling depressed and suicidal?

I prepped for a day or so and just as I was on my way to tell one of the officers my tale of woe, one of the white boys who was gonna try this same approach came walking in. He didn't look too happy.

"Hmmmm," I say, "you not headed home?"

He shakes his head, not talkin'.

I look down and notice his boots have no shoelaces. "What happened to your laces?"

That's when he tells me they don't send you home for wanting to commit suicide. They just take your laces so you don't hang yourself.

There went my plan! Resigned to make the most of a bad situation, I tried to shape up, but I was hands down the weakest one in Basic Training. Seriously, I could move my hips like an acrobat—maybe thanks to years of having sex like a grown person—but I had two sticks for arms. Felt like I was the weakest soldier in the world—at least as far as upper-body strength.

Was I 'bout to get my ass kicked to Kingdom Come by superiors and fellow recruits? The problem was real.

The only solution, learned from my time in the City, was to channel the lion roar in my voice to a level I'd never had to harness in the past and act so crazy nobody would try to mess with me. The goal was to have them all so scared of me *before* they made a move.

If any of the other recruits were hanging out and playing near me in the barracks, I'd talk deep and *loud* and *go off* saying, "HEYYYYYY! STOP! NOWWWWWWW! Stop playin' round my bunk. For real and everything! If y'all don't stop, I'ma SLAP EVERYONE IN HERE!"

That is conviction and commitment.

Everybody backed off. They were really scared. That is until one day when this one big, strong, cocky, white boy decided to call my bluff. He looked me dead in my eyes first and pushed my battle buddy. So naturally I stood up and was about to *blast* this bully when he cut me off.

"COLLEY! I'm tired of you thinking you run everything! I ain't scared of you!"

And as he took a step I silently prayed, *Oh, please don't let this cock-strong white boy push me 'cause I'm gonna fly so far they gonna send me to the Air Force.* It would have been ugly. Instead, I did the most practical, nonviolent thing I could devise in the moment. I looked at him and said in a normal voice, "Hey, man, I got no problem with you. This is my partner. I'm gonna give you a pass but the next time you hit him, you and me are gonna go one-on-one and it won't end well for you." He folded his arms, undecided. I went on, "Like I said, I'm gonna stay out of it for now and I ain't gonna jump you this time. But watch your hands in the future."

For a few moments he stood there and then made up his mind that fighting me wasn't worth it. He backed down. Little did he know, boy, I was holding my breath the whole time.

In hindsight, I could see how incidents like that were valuable for my whole future, for teaching me how *not* to be intimidated. In other ways, I can see God had a plan for having me stick out Basic Training that I didn't appreciate right away. Ironically, I probably showed the most growth and leadership in our unit. I'd hear other guys in my barracks calling home to their moms or other family members and I'd miss having my momma to call. I'd imagine her telling me, "Stay smart and pay attention."

That's what I tried to do. In the process, the Army taught me much more than I had expected—especially discipline and teamwork.

Attention to detail was something else that I got from Basic Training. You didn't just drop down to do a push-up. You had to think about placement, posture, breathing, core strength. The Army also taught me the benefits of routine—that became a lasting part of how I lived from then on. Things like how to monitor and oversee your schedule every day, how you make your bed, the importance of decent nutrition and an exercise regimen, and how to spruce up your appearance with small details. The concept of having some kind of uniform made sense to me. In the civilian world, you could still walk and dress with the confidence and command of an officer, even if you weren't one. The experience was great training for becoming a parent, too. I realized that structure, responsibilities, and routine give children a sense of security—especially when they receive praise for jobs well done. Bottom line, the fact is that I liked learning and I was fascinated by how systems that required teamwork and discipline required leadership. The Army had been around forever and there was a method to what I had first thought was madness.

All of that said, the Army was not for me in the long term. The thought that I would have to serve again after high school kept me up at night. But I had to graduate from Basic Training to get my check and that was going to require running a 15k race with a backpack full of shovels and other heavy tools. In my last-resort effort to survive, I cheated. Instead of equipment in my backpack, I stuffed my blanket in there and threw water on my face like I was sweating.

Before the run, I had gone to my sergeant to see if I could get out of it because of my scoliosis. It wasn't something that had ever bothered me but on my physical the doctor had said that I had a mild case of it. The sergeant seemed to see right through me and told me that I'd have to suck it up and do the run. So, I was sure he'd be watching me like a hawk and ask to search my backpack.

Glory hallelujah, I was wrong. In fact, he was impressed at how I made it through the marsh and offered to let me ride in the back of the truck instead of having to return to camp on foot. Once I cleared the 15k with flying colors, despite the trouble I could have gotten into, I went through my Basic Training graduation as a proud soldier.

The motivation to stick with it came from a new awareness that making it through wasn't just about me. I was starting to learn to understand the importance of *who*—the baby on the way—which helped me find my passion. But I still knew that even if I made it through training, there was no way I could do the real Army. I needed a plan B, maybe by getting a Pell Grant and other student loans for college. First, though, I had to find a way to get out of my commitment to starting AIT (Advanced Individual Training) after graduation. The scoliosis wasn't severe enough, unfortunately.

After turning over all the stones, I decided to read through the fine print about what I'd signed up for. The line that jumped out at me specified that no felon could sign to get into the armed services. I couldn't believe my eyes. Because I was a minor, my daddy had signed me up. Nobody asked him if he legally could do that. In fact, Vincent Colley, at this point in 2005, already had a felony conviction.

Unable to hide my relief, I march up to my drill sergeant and tell him that I'm not required by law to report to duty after high school graduation.

"You think you can outsmart the system, Colley? Well, you are WRONG. If you don't report the day after you graduate, we will lock you up. And if that's what it takes to wipe that smile off your face, I will make it my personal business to do so."

I smile even bigger, telling him, "You do that, and I'll tell everyone how y'all are letting felons sign up underage sons to serve in the Guard." After he blows smoke out his nose and ears, I explain the facts to him and he tries to argue but a superior officer interrupts and tells me, "We'll look into it."

They did and the next thing I knew I graduated with pay for my Basic Training and was given an honorable discharge.

I arrived back home just in time to welcome the young prince Tony Colley into this world. The first time I held him in my arms, he looked up at me with a serious scowl on his face and at the same time laughter in his eyes. Tilquisha was beautiful in motherhood. She was never happier than just being with her baby.

Tony reminded me of the sunflower in our yard years earlier. My baby couldn't talk yet but I understood that he was here to watch over me as much as I was gonna watch over him. I couldn't let him down.

School's Out

My senior year was a stressful blur. Looking back, I can see that it was the final year of my youth and I should have tried to enjoy it more. But I was just focused on graduating and getting started on handling the demands of real life. This is terrible to say but, in hindsight, my experience of high school was sort of like being in teenage day care. Now that I'm raising my own kids, I see what I missed and realize the different ways I could have done more to take advantage of that time period. And I do my best to make sure my kids don't make those same mistakes.

All that said, during my last year I was simply laser-focused on getting out and finding a way to uphold my responsibilities of taking care of Queet and our new son.

In my rush to move on, I took my time in school for granted—and especially some truly caring teachers who believed in me. Many of them chose their professions because they were passionate about teaching and even more passionate about who they were teaching for. The fact that I had chosen to become a teacher after college goes to show that I was inspired by teachers who genuinely wanted me to succeed.

I had one teacher, Mrs. Drake, who I made laugh so much she'd make exceptions for me all the time. She once tried to flunk me—which I thought was actually a ploy to keep me around another year to make her laugh. We had all kinds of banter. There was this one time, for example, when someone snitched on me and told her I copied answers for a test, and Mrs. Drake confronted me to ask if that was true. My reaction was to throw her off by responding, "Do the math, that wouldn't make sense."

"I know you're not telling me the truth."

I shrugged and asked sheepishly, "What am I supposed to do, tell on myself?"

That time she held back her laughter and gave me a lecture about living up to my potential. Once I became a teenage dad, I think she accepted that I was trying to do better but couldn't quite manage to study. From then on, she cut me some slack. She would even pretend not to notice on test days that the straight-A girls would let me copy off their homework and tests.

On final exam day, some of the less charitable students called me out in front of Mrs. Drake. I wasn't gonna blow her cover so when she folded her arms and became very stern, I hung my head and shrugged my shoulders. She scowled at me, saying, "Dewayne Colley, I don't trust you. Go up to my desk, bring your test with you, and fill it out there."

My overall grade was already in the 60s. Now I was in serious trouble. I had not studied a lick. Sitting there shaking my head, I looked over on one side of the teacher's desk and saw something that told me help was on the way! Sitting right there, plain as day, was her grading sheet—*with all the answers!* It was all's well that ends well . . . until one of the smart, know-it-all girls came up and saw me filling in the answers from the grading sheet. Her name was Angel but she was clearly the Devil on this day.

"Wayne is cheating!" Angel said. "Wayne is cheating!"

Our teacher had no choice but to walk over, kinda slow, as she put on a whole *appalled* attitude. She acted so shocked as she said dramatically, "Are you serious, Dewayne? You're cheating?!"

I played along, acting just as dramatic and sheepish and apologetic as you can imagine. Pretty soon, everybody in the class was falling out of their seats laughing. It was my first skit! Call it my first inkling that comedy could make me money one day.

I managed to fill in enough of the right answers that I brought my grade up and she gave me extra credit enough to pass her class. She later told me that she was hard on me because she believed I could do really well if I applied myself. She also said that she thought I was going to do great things—but not if I didn't stop getting in my own way.

High school did teach me the power of leveraging popularity and charm, which I put to use in building an audience later, when I finally got on social media.

Another teacher who cared was Mrs. Johnson. She never made anything personal. She praised good work and criticized bad work. I liked that. I thought of her as a role model. Mrs. Johnson did give me advice one time, asking what my plans were after graduation. Out of character for her, she told me, "Don't stay in Millen. You're a big fish in a little pond now. But you should get out there. Just don't get stuck here."

And then there was the teacher who never liked me: Coach Haines, who had nothing encouraging to say. He hated my guts. No exaggeration. "You are a cancer to people around here," he said to me a short time before graduation. He went on to say that people followed me and that was bad because they did it for the wrong things. Normally, I'd shake a comment like that off. I understood that people will hate you because they see something you have that they want. Or they see something in you that reminds them of a part of themselves that they dislike.

The best way I could put his comments into context was to see that I was being given a preview of how the real world was about to get *really* real. At graduation, I felt it weighing on me. By coincidence, Tilquisha's last name was close to Colley and we were sitting next to each other. A thought crossed my mind, so I leaned over and asked, "Have you seen your period this month?"

Queet shook her head no. She'd missed the last two months, in fact.

Quietly, I sat there and counted out what that probably meant. We were going to have a second child, most likely in December. I was already enrolled in East Georgia State College in Swainsboro, about a forty-minute commute. Classes were starting in August.

My Social Security checks had just ended. My Basic Training money was spent. My college Pell Grant check wasn't going to arrive until classes began. And no legit job was on the horizon.

The solution was to start hustling right away. My uncle Cleave took me under his wing and gave me a crash course in marketing. He had once taught me how to kiss a woman's feet and now he was showing me how to get on my feet.

The thing I remember most about making that decision that night at graduation was how everyone else was celebrating being done with high school and throwing their caps in the air. "WOOOO-HOOOO!" Not me. I was off on my own, lost in thought, calculating the cost of more baby formula and more Pampers and reminding myself of the lesson that it's not so much *what* you do but *who* you do it for.

Lean into Your Passions

Passion is like summer lightning. You don't even need a raging storm to light it up. When something comes along that makes you feel passionate, by all means do everything you can to explore the possibilities and capture the lightning in a bottle. Fill that bottle up with interests and ideas that will make your life rich and colorful.

Not everything you put in your bottled lightning collection has to be your job—or your side hustle or the calling that you'd be doing if you could. On the other hand, when you choose to make your passion a full-time endeavor, that's where the grind and the sacrifices come in. That's also where you may want to ask yourself *who* you feel passionate about grinding for.

Passion in general is magnetic. The characters in my video stories are defined by their passions, for better and for worse. Take Buddy. He doesn't quite get it. The most important *who* in his passion is himself, first, and whatever woman he is trying to entice, second, and that can change depending on *whoever* he is with at the moment. Buddy's *what* is his real estate and other investments and there's something to be learned from that. He may not be so likable, in part because he is so straightforward. "Chase the money, don't chase the woman." After all, according to him, "You need to let the woman chase your money. It's less work for you."

Drip is passionate about everything. He knows the difference between being passionate about *what* he does and being more passionate about *who* he loves. Drip always confesses everything by swearing "On everything I love," and by that he means his Drip-lette, that is, his daughter. When he finally gets to have a relationship with her and become the father he always wanted to be, he listens hard to her question, "How you get this money?" He is not happy when she goes on to tell him that she heard from a friend's mother that he's hustling. He assures her that he is not, but from then on, he is more determined than ever to prove he is a legit rapper.

Drip has his own philosophy about passion: "Yuh, you gots to be passionate on what you love and make sure it love you back! Look at the prefix of passion—it's 'pass.' And if you have it, you will pass anyone less passionate. Yuh, yuh, and when you don't have that passion, you gonna let everything pass you up."

Good point. You might have Drip-lets and Drip-lettes of your own. Your *who* might be your family, your community, your mentors. They are blessings to be loved because they bring out your strengths.

You'll probably find that the list of people who motivate you to be your best can change over the years. Family is always right up front for me. But I feel passionate to this day about people who believed in me when no one else did—and my grind is a way to remind them that I was worth investing in. The same goes in reverse for the people who didn't believe in me.

Some of your best motivation can come from people who do not have your best interests at heart. They would never admit it, but the idea of you winning in spite of them keeps them up all night.

That's all the more reason for you to win at a scale your haters can't even fathom—and for you to leave them sputtering in your dust.

CHAPTER 7

CAN'T CATCH ME

Learn to Stop While You Are Ahead— Because Luck Will Run Out

Most all of us at some point in our lives have said—"I shoulda quit when I was ahead." It usually comes out right after we find ourselves stuck too deep in a bad situation and can't get out. We might have even seen and ignored some clear warning signs and consciously chosen not to take the off-ramp.

Whether it's with a relationship not meant to last, or a business investment that sounded too good to be true, or an addictive habit many of us wanted to try just *once* and then get out, we often jump right in without thinking ahead and then stay longer than we should. The better it is at first and the faster the rewards come in the beginning, the more we delay stopping it. We think the benefits we're getting are gonna outweigh the costs, at least in the short run. It's all starting to flow so nicely in our favor for a little while that we begin to rationalize, and we ignore the voice of common sense, telling us that we are tempting fate.

Why? Why don't we listen?

Mainly, it's because we think we're smart enough to get out the minute the problems become real. We think we can keep everything under control. Or, it's because we convince ourselves that we're just lucky. That's where we are wrong. Luck will mess with our better judgment every time. They don't call it "dumb luck" for *nuthin*. If you get lucky in a negative world, even if you are there for positive motives, you don't want to stay in too long. And that's when you are really gonna need to *learn to stop while you are ahead, because luck is sure to run out.*

For all the lessons I learned early in my life, this wasn't one of them. It took many, many times of pushing my luck for me to finally choose to stop when I was ahead. So I'm with you if you find this to be one of the harder lessons to truly take to heart.

I was so careful to avoid the curse of getting addicted to drugs or alcohol that I didn't pay attention to other potential addictions. Specifically: gambling. I used to love the feeling of winning so much, I had to keep going. It wasn't about the money, really, but about the thrill of the risk and being lucky enough to defy the odds. *Oooooh*, it's addictive when you think luck is on your side so much that you can beat the system. But after a few times of losing money that I didn't have to lose, I learned that the only way to beat the system is to stop while you are ahead.

That's a healthy habit.

When you win in the casino, instead of doubling down, why not cash out your chips, and walk out? Just walk out. Money in your pocket! You are not rolling the dice one more time. You are stopping while you are ahead. And it feels good to outsmart the temptation to think you can keep on being lucky when, in fact, you know your luck will run out eventually.

Sometimes I don't follow my own advice. That's why every year I give myself a gambling allowance and only go to the casino once or twice for the whole year. And I lose so bad it's embarrassing. I once lost thirty grand at blackjack and had to cut myself off for the rest of the year. It's gotten to where I don't ever go to the casino to win—because I know I'm gonna lose.

I'm actually scared to get too lucky at gambling, because *that's* the bigger addiction. If I ever do win a big lick, I'm never gonna quit.

When it comes to hustling, I knew early on why it is important to stop while you're ahead. I saw that lesson in action with Pops and my uncles and other family members. Most of them didn't get out when they had a chance. And I was determined not to let that happen to me. How? By deciding to keep my business small-time and short-term.

Well, you might ask, why get into hustling in the first place? It was because, in my situation, the consequences of Fast Money outweighed the consequences of No Money. Maybe it was the City slickness in me that made me think I was too fast to get caught. Maybe it was my Kountry simple side that made me think I could slow-talk my way out of trouble. Yeah, I can see you right now thinking, *Why didn't you take your own advice of what you just said?* And you are right. But I still had to learn about how the faster rewards come, the harder it is to stop.

Anyway, the plan was to stop once I had enough to get a jump on child support, help put myself through college to get that teaching degree, and bankroll my rap career. The possibility of getting locked up at some point was always there. But that was reality. Besides, the truth is that I actually was lucky out of the gate. Too lucky.

Until a turning point came when I wasn't anymore.

Welcome to the Traphouse

East Georgia State College in Swainsboro, Georgia, was down the road a hop, skip, and jump southwest of Millen. About forty minutes or less, depending on how fast I was speeding. The town of Swainsboro is about double the population of Millen—but that's mainly because it's a college town, and the college itself has an enrollment of 3,500, give or take. So it wasn't like I'd gone away to a different culture to get an education or to be exposed to new ideas. But, still, it was interesting to see the more sophisticated attitudes of students I met on campus—even though most, like me, were from Kountry towns and commuted to attend class.

When I started my first semester, I noticed right off that after the money from a Pell Grant got spent on tuition and books, the little bit left over barely covered gas, let alone the cost of supporting a hungry toddler and a second son due in a few months. Hustling on the side helped, but I wanted to avoid selling in Millen and I was smart enough not to deal on campus. Instead, I decided to test the waters in Statesboro. It was like striking gold. So much opportunity, even for a side hustle.

A lot of folks have heard "Statesboro Blues"—made famous by the Allman Brothers' recording and named by *Rolling Stone* as the number 9 greatest song of all time. In fact, it was written and recorded in 1928 by Blind Willie McTell, a Black blues guitar player who grew up in Statesboro. The Allman Brothers put out their record in 1970, way before my time, but it made me proud when I heard it later.

Statesboro, the biggest town anywhere near us, could even brag about having a mall. That alone put it at a different level from all the other towns around. It was only a stone's throw over yonder from Millen—about a thirty-mile drive in a southeast direction. Statesboro has a population of over 36,000, with another 20,000 students at Georgia Southern University. Even though the campus was smack-dab in the middle of town, there was an invisible wall around it that separated the 'hood from the university. And that wall was run by the Statesboro Police Department. This was a whole new world for me.

Then again, I'd lived in the City of Atlanta and knew that Statesboro was still Kountry. In Millen we knew who we were. We lived our down-home truth, but folks in Statesboro thought they were City—and *that* made them even more Kountry. And yet, I knew the big Kountry town was the perfect stepping-stone for my larger-than-life future. At age eighteen, going on nineteen, something told me my future would lead through Statesboro.

This didn't mean I had given up on getting a college education. Except . . . well, I was a little lax in showing up for all my classes my first couple of weeks. Realizing I'd better get up to speed, I was lucky that most of the professors let me slide on in when I did show. Not all of them, though. One professor stopped me in my tracks as I was headed to the back.

"Who are you?"

"Dewayne Colley," I answered and stood confidently near the door as he checked the class roster.

"Nope," the professor said. "You're not in the class."

I held out my registration slip, showing him. "This says I am."

"You got kicked out."

"I can't get kicked out. I never came."

Behind me I could hear a few laughs. But the professor was not charmed. He put a firm hand on my shoulder and guided me right out the class. Before I could say another word, he closed the door in my face!

Madder that a wet hen, I marched up to the academic counseling office and complained to a counselor, "This man just kicked me out of his class."

The counselor pointed out that I had missed the first two weeks of the course and it was too late to make up the work.

"Y'all don't want me to learn! It's because I'm Black."

The counselor wasn't going to budge. Those were the rules. And that was that.

Seeing as I didn't get kicked out of the other classes, I did the work and caught up. Fortunately, I'm a quick learner. My first year in college taught me a little about a lot of things but the eye-opener was that in the real world nobody is going to pin awards on you for having potential and give you tough love pep talks about applying yourself. Now it's on you.

The rest of the first semester flew by. Between classes, schoolwork, my weekend hustle in Statesboro and in Millen, I was only squeaking by financially. The only answer I could see was to up the hustling. The catch-22 was, to do that I'd need to come up with a larger outlay of cash. Resolved to figure it out, I started to play with a couple of ideas—certain that one of them would pan out.

In that confident state of mind, in December 2006, Queet and I happily welcomed Temar into the world. He proved from the start to have a will of iron. Tony had been an easygoing, mellow, loving baby. Temar was that way, too—only sometimes, even as an infant, he'd look at me like, *Well, let's go!*

One night I confided in Queet how badly I wanted to get us out of Millen so we didn't have to struggle so hard.

She saw no reason for us to leave our hometown. Queet said, "If we got to struggle, it's okay, 'cause we can struggle together."

I knew she meant it with *nuthin* but love. Yet I realized then that we had two very different visions for the future. That realization lit a fire in me and I knew I had to *turn up*. But how?

Well, in a moment of great timing, I learned that there was a trap-house in Statesboro run by one of Queet's family members who said I could take it over—as long as I came up with the rent. A "trap" is what you call a private house or apartment, as opposed to a corner or the back of a club or some public place, where you can go buy drugs. This trap in Statesboro was an older house, in the 'hood—not a bad loca-tion, but Queet's relative was letting it go because he hadn't been able to make it profitable.

No way was I gonna pass up a lucky break like this! With only a bit of guilt, I used some of my student loan to cover the costs of taking over the rent.

My brother Arby, right out of high school, too, became a partner in the business. He was all in favor of me taking the lead and putting my own marketing talents into action. I put out the word that we would only sell recreational quantities and never crack, heroin, or pills. And I made sure that the product was A1, not cut with anything toxic or dangerous. I wanted customers to know that their safety was our busi-ness, too. I'd bring out a scale to measure their purchases and the buyers would look surprised.

"So you know I'm not cheating you." It was that important for them to see they were getting a fair deal.

Being in charge of having my own business was cool, I gotta say. And much of what I learned helped lay the groundwork for other businesses that were ahead of me. Sure, it was only a traphouse, but I took pride in it not being a dump and even being kind of inviting. Arby and my other partner agreed that if there were women coming around, especially, we should keep the place clean. Of course, we were careful not to create too much of a party atmosphere.

Yet I couldn't resist parking my yellow and red–striped 1995 Crown Victoria out in front. Momma Doog had spoiled me by giving me this old car for an early graduation gift. That came about because her employers gave her a black Kia, which she didn't love but had to drive, so I got her beloved Crown Vic, which was red at the time. After painting it yellow with red racing stripes and adding a custom yellow leather top to match, I was spoiled again when Momma Doog bought 22-inch rims, which I immediately also painted yellow. Momma Doog and Jackie probably went into debt with their generosity to me. I used to wonder if this was one more way Momma was sending me gifts from heaven—through them.

Arby's mom had given him money from her Social Security check when he was in his senior year and he'd gotten an older, green Crown Victoria with 22-inch rims, too. When we parked our cars side by side in front of the trap, that was all the advertisement we needed. It was like McDonald's golden arches had just been lit up. Everybody started talking about us. "Who are these two new dope boys with matching cars?" Before we'd even sold a thing, everybody assumed we were already *on*.

Word spread like wildfire. And they all wanted to come shop with us.

Some of my marketing concepts came from years of watching my daddy and my uncles but also from watching commercials. If I was looking, say, for a trusted insurance agency, I'd want the guy who pulled up in a Mercedes. No offense to the guy who pulls up in a Honda, but it's natural to want to do business with a person who appears to be successful already. A flashy, fast car can really set you apart. Even if you might not want to be set apart in certain ways.

In the long run, hustling taught me a lot about not depending on luck but about really being on top of the numbers. I learned what Return On Investment (ROI) means and why you want to earn more than you spend. I learned the difference between profit (what you have after you deduct your expenses) and how much inventory you sold outright versus the value of unsold product. I learned not to push something on somebody that I knew deep down was bad for them. That may sound strange in a line of work like dealing but I imagined that I was like a bartender—serving drinks to the customers but not overselling the liquor, even cutting the drinkers off if they're asking for more but getting out of control.

Besides, pushing to make a sale of anything was never my style. Instead, I tried to show how I valued their business and cared about their satisfaction. That's how you get repeat business and word of mouth. Customer service was key, especially when selling to clientele who were older than me. I never forgot my Kountry manners—"Yessir, thank you fo stoppin' by," and "Of course, ma'am, let me get that for you."

I earned enough in the first two weeks to pay for tuition, books, and fees, and give money to Queet and look out for my sisters. Business boomed. We were so busy, Arby and I recruited some cousins and relatives of my baby mama to help out.

After a couple months, the trap was practically running itself and I was able to get to my classes and spend time with my baby boys. My share of the profit was up to $2,000 a week and it was all going good. I thought then about stopping while we were ahead, as I knew it was only a matter of time before the police would get wind of us. Remember what I said about not listening to my own advice? Well, it did cross my mind that those cars could get us in trouble, but then I'd let that concern go. So far, so good.

At least that's what I thought.

You know, Fast Money can be as seductive as coochie. Sometimes more. It will make you forget your common sense. I almost felt untouchable. Then, in March, for the first time one night, I got spotted by the Statesboro police while I was sitting in a friend's car and they came up to the windows, asking for our IDs. I didn't have mine on me but gave them my name.

When they went back to their car, I put what I was carrying on me in my sock and was chillin', thinking they'd run our names, find *nuthin*, and let us go. Much to my shock, when I looked back, I saw they had a K9 truck pulling up. Then I did what Drip would have done. That is, *don't act nervous and get out of there as fast as you can.*

These were *not* the Millen police. There was no friendly banter or cat-and-mouse game. They just suspected something and when I ran, they thundered after me. But I was faster. They were so far behind, the dog barking and all, they didn't see me at the point when I spotted an old busted up, abandoned van and threw my stash under it. Then I sprinted around the back of the traphouse and started to get into my Crown Victoria—only my hands were shaking so badly, I couldn't get the door open. Just then, the policeman and the dog, both out of breath, came around the corner.

"Scuse me, sir," the officer said, "have you seen a guy named Dewayne Colley running through here?"

I thought, *Is this police asking me about ME?*

The dog was growling real low. He knew.

I took a deep breath, yawned to hide how winded I was, and told him, "Yeah, I saw a guy, I think it was him. I seen him go up the street. He ran that way—" I pointed into the night. Then I got in the car and drove back to where we were first spotted, back by my friend, who was facedown on the hood of his car as the police interrogated him about where I was.

I drove by slowly, looked him dead in the eye, letting him know he better not say anything.

A week later, thinking the coast was clear, I got in my Ronald McDonald–looking, dope boy car and raced over to the old van. Glory be! My bag was still there. Nobody had thought to look under an old raggedy, broke-down camper van. People were out on the street and I just couldn't help from bragging to everyone around—"Y'all coulda had free dope but you didn't even bother to search after the police left!"

Everyone was mad. I shouldn't have rubbed it in. The fact that they didn't find it was another piece of luck. Instead of quitting while I was ahead, I now had a "can't catch me" attitude.

It only took a week for me to be proven wrong. This time, I was in my grandmomma's car with my brother Arby. The police pulled us over because the car's tags were missing the name of the county where the car was registered. They ran both of our IDs this time. After a painful half hour, they came back with confident expressions. They had called the same officer who I had run from the week before and were now pleased to inform me that I was going to be spending the night in jail for obstruction of officers.

Because the arrest was my first, after booking me at the jailhouse, they let me go home once I posted bond. Another lucky break.

The "can't catch me" tune kept playing in my ears.

A week later, I'm riding with a friend who is driving my car, and we're going to do a drop-off. The police pull us over and we both have drugs on our laps.

I turn to him, saying, "You gotta run, 'cause I ran last week and can't get caught."

"Naw, man, I can't." With that he tries to swallow the cocaine. Inside the bags and everything.

"Wait!" Before he gags to death, I say, "Gimme that." I grab his bags and mine, and go bounding from the car, cursing myself for pushing my luck.

Moving from raw instinct, I go speeding down the street, arms pumping and hands in motion. They're close behind me but, again, it's dark, and as soon as I come around a corner I veer into a trailer park and choose the first tall trailer I can see. Like a ballerina, poised on one foot in tippy-toe—with one hand uplifted to the sky and a toe pointed in the air, for balance—I sling the drugs up and onto the top of the trailer.

From there, I hide in the bushes, which, unluckily, are a dense grove of brambles and sticker bushes. Now I can't move and want them to find me and free me.

When a female officer shows up, I call to her: "Ma'am, I'm over here." She helps me out, and I emerge from the bushes, scratched and bloody, with one shoe in my hand.

The other officers, all male, rush over and she shines a light in my face. One of the guys says, "Isn't that the same one who ran last week?" Someone else says, "Say it isn't so."

The female officer says, "You shoulda run faster." And gives me a look, like she's rooting for me.

More police show up with their drug-sniffing dog. I've never seen this amount of law enforcement at one time. *Mannnnnn,* my heart is *pounding* as that dog sniffs all around the trailer on the ground—and then moves on.

The Statesboro police are furious that they've got me but can't find anything on me. So they keep me for seven miserable days in the jail cell. Finally, once again, I get lucky. Once they admit they can't find anything, and let me go.

The police didn't find my stash on top of the trailer because they never thought of looking up high. They needed a drug-sniffing cat instead of a dog.

As soon as I got out of jail, I made a phone call and managed to get two of the traphouse's regular helpers to get a ladder and go out to the trailer and climb up to see if the coke was still there. I went with them and held the ladder.

"Well?" I asked, as they climbed down.

"We found it," one of them said. The other one added, "We coulda kept it but you trust us and we couldn't do that to you."

It was only fair for me to give them a share for their help and honesty. Getting anything back was one more stroke of luck. By this point, though, I really did start to get the message that I was pushing it. Common sense alone should have told me that it was time to get out while I was ahead. Right then and there.

At least I realized that the trap was getting hot and I should stay away, letting the other guys run it. It was a good time to *start* to get out and that's what I decided to do. Except . . . in a couple weeks I went from $2,000 to $5. Broke again.

My next step was to turn to a supplier who was willing to front me some product. It's never been my approach to buy anything on credit and I had some misgivings. So, after I sold half of what he fronted me, I repaid him, then fronted the other half to the traphouse—$1,700 of which I still owed the supplier.

A few days went by and I was home, getting ready to get out of bed and go to Statesboro—to check out my traphouse and get my money—when the phone rang. It was my sister Shavonne.

"Did you hear about the trap?"

"Naw, I'm on my way there."

She gave me the news that the police had busted it. This was awful. One of my cousins and one of Queet's relatives were there and had to go to jail! And I still owed the supplier $1,700.

And *that's* when my hustling luck really ran out. God was cutting me some slack, though, because I could have been there. Instead, I walked away from trapping without anything worse on my record than the two misdemeanors.

But now I was, for real, broke. Zero dollars.

All of a sudden, I really, really got the lesson about getting out while you are ahead. Fast Money was no longer calling to me. At this point, I had to think that some slow money might not be so bad.

Forget hustling on the side. I was gonna go out and get a legit job. Some Working-Man Money sounded most welcome. You know—Every Week Money.

I finished the second semester of college but didn't apply for assistance for the next year. Looking back, I regret that I didn't stick it out and get my degree. Then again, I try not to live with regrets but to trust that I'm learning everything I'm supposed to learn at the exact right time. The working world was about to prove that.

Seduction of Fast Money

You are probably wondering right now how I went from stopping while I was ahead in April of my nineteenth year to being out in the field five months later in Millen, hiding from the law.

Well, the story had a twist and turn or two. For the first time, listen, I was no longer blinded by the promise of being lucky or the seduction of Fast Money. My real problem was 1) *bills* and 2) underestimating just how bad Brad Adams had it in for me.

Let me tell you how that all played out. Through a friend of my cousin Jackie—or "Jack," as I call her—I heard about a job at MI (Metal Industries). This was one of the last big employers in Millen that offered good-paying jobs. Like $1,000 every couple of weeks, plus benefits. So, I went in and applied. Joe, the supervisor, seemed to like me and more or less said I had the job.

I left there praising Jesus and holding my head high. Working-Man and Family Man Money!

Then I heard *nuthin*. They never called me back. I asked Jack to ask her friend, who didn't know anything. So I went back there, in person, to find out what the deal was.

Being direct, I said, "Hey, Joe, why y'all ain't call me back, man?"

He said, "We checked around and it came back that you're a known drug dealer."

Straight-up, I told him that was true in the past but I was not in that anymore. "I'm trying to do right, man," I told him. "Give me a chance. I'm gonna be the hardest worker here."

Joe took that chance and gave me a job, and that was being lucky in a positive world. The job was boring but required some skill—feeding glass into a machine. But I was *into* it. I studied the workers who were careful, efficient, and productive, and made it my goal to be even better. The boss went on vacation when I was getting started and when he returned, I saw him watching me all eagle-eyed.

He was amazed. If I don't say so myself, I was *good*. He couldn't believe how fast I was and told me so. I will never forget the awesome feeling of being recognized for hard work and skill. About a week later, we had a meeting with other supervisors and workers and he started by saying, "You know if we ever get behind in production and don't get our orders out on time, it won't be because of Dewayne Colley."

Hearing my name was humbling. I smiled and nodded.

He went on, saying, "I have watched him from the start. And I'm so proud of this young man."

When I got off work, I zipped right home to tell Queet and spend some daddy time with little Tony and Temar. I'm a working man, that's what's up! Life was Kountry simple. Over those early weeks I knew money was tight and we didn't have as much coming in as we were used to getting from the streets. Somehow, I wasn't paying close attention but making ends meet was so hard. I realized by week four or so that, after taxes, my paycheck was $700—for two weeks! Then I started to pay the bills, extra because of fixing my car, and rent and food. That's when it hit, *Damn, if I pay all these bills, I'll have nuthin left!* Plus, my baby mama's mother was dropping hints about me not being a good enough provider.

She had to add, "And quit slammin' that door when you leave in the mornin so early!"

Upset, I went to talk to my cousin Jack about how I'm workin' so hard, never getting ahead. "This ain't livin'!" I complained.

Jack told me, "That's how it go, bro."

"Aw, hell naw!"

Then, trying like crazy *not* to hustle again, instead of paying my bills, I went and gambled that $700. Lost it all. For someone smart, I was making every wrong move.

And that's how I ended up hustling again. The one sensible thing I did was keep my legit day job at MI. But I was back in the game. I did keep a low profile this time, though—in and around Millen. Cut down the flash and did my thing quietly. But the streets knew. I'd become the Man in the City in Statesboro and that gave me even more prestige in my hometown.

Millen police knew that, too, unfortunately. The Colley brothers were considered suspicious outlaws mostly because of our cars. The funny thing is we were such small-time hustlers that it made them even madder they couldn't catch us. The moral of the story is that you should always avoid getting attention in the wrong world.

For seven weeks, I pushed my luck.

Well, you probably remember what happened next—how, after the police found the stash I had thrown out in the field, I was facing prosecution for possession with the intent to distribute. My two earlier arrests in Statesboro had only been misdemeanors. This was now a felony.

Sitting in that Millen jail cell for three days was a low point. I'm not gonna lie. But I had to go back to all the lessons of my life, remembering to stay up (or at least act like it), reconnect to my truth of who I was and what I believed, and trust my conviction that even in the darkest hours, there is always hope. That little bit of hope caused me to realize, more clearly than ever, that help was on its way. When I started to look around and pay attention, help started to show up.

First, it was from my cousin/godsister Jackie, who posted bond, putting up land in her name instead of money. That was a blessing. Another saving grace was that, until I was indicted, I could count on the job at MI. For two months, I kept to the grindstone, feeding glass into machinery with a heart full of gratitude and faith that I was going to be given guidance no matter how the ax of the indictment fell.

Before that even happened, though, my boss at MI called me into his office to say they were letting me go. He quickly explained it had *nuthin* to do with me. The plant was closing down and all nonessential workers were being let go.

I was a month away from my twentieth birthday. Tony was two-and-a-half by now and Temar was almost one. The fear that kept me up at night was that I was gonna get locked up and not be able to provide for them. In the meantime, I put the word out to everyone that I was looking for legit work. In no time, I heard back from Momma Doog's other daughter that her husband said he could get me hired on at Caddell, a contractor that supplied laborers in the environmental division for Georgia Power & Electric Company.

Mannnnnn, I praised the Lord for the opportunity and got hired so fast it about made my head spin. The work was physically demanding, even dangerous, but I got to travel all around the state, cleaning up oil spills, fixing transformers, maintaining electrical wiring, and being like a Save the Day Working Man whenever there was trouble in the power company world. This was more than a lucky break. It was almost miraculous.

A couple of weeks after I started at Georgia Power, we were on a lunch break one day and I saw a homeless man who seemed to appear out of nowhere. He was begging and it hurt my heart to see him. Whatever his story was, I had no idea. But I wondered if maybe he had kids of his own and was just doing what he had to do. I went over, said hello, gave him several bills, and wished him well.

My coworkers gave me a hard time. One guy said, "C'mon, Wayne, how come you gave that homeless man some money?" Another added, "Yeah, they can work, too. The homeless are just lazy."

"It ain't about doing for him," I explained. "I did it for me. For my heart."

Nobody understood.

"Y'all wait," I said. "God's fixin' to show y'all something. It was in my spirit to do. That's all."

To be honest, I don't know why I said that.

But, *sho'nuff,* a true miracle was lying in wait. The next day, I got a call from human resources at MI that there was a check for me I needed to come by and pick up.

No other explanation. I figured it was a small severance check for working there that I wasn't given when they first laid me off. I told my coworkers about the call and said my grandmomma was gonna go pick up the check for me.

"Probably around $500," I guessed. Or at least I was praying.

The guys were impressed.

"Well," I said, "I can go pay a few bills."

Then Grandmomma Mary called me. She began, "Boy, God is sho with you." The check was *not* $500. It was a check for $3,000!

But wait. There is more.

Not many days later, I received an early tax refund check. Back when I had taken out the school loans, I'd withheld money to pay taxes and then when I went to work, I filed right away. The IRS messed around, like we say in the Kountry, and sent me a refund check for $7,000!

Help had arrived. This was $10,000.00! More money from working nine-to-five jobs and living in the legit world than I had ever, ever had at one time. The timing couldn't have been better. That money was gonna let me take wonderful care of my family *and,* sooner or later, let me pay for my lawyer.

I had seen the light. And would continue to do so. At least for the next two years.

We All Learn

We all learn at different speeds. My hope is that you will learn from my journey and if you are in the wrong world, you'll decide to stop while you are ahead. We don't always get second and third chances, either, and, as they say, but for the grace of God, you might not get out in time.

Look at Drip. He can't get out. He is addicted to the lifestyle. He only knows Fast Money. He'll never leave the game because he can't play by any rules other than his own. Buddy's got similar issues. Buddy may have gotten his money in a legit way—he's not really talking about that. It gives him his stroll, even so. But Buddy uses that money for sex to replace the emptiness of never having real love. If a sugar daddy really takes care of a woman, who takes care of him, that's not the worst thing. The problem with Buddy is, if she tries to get out, he'll have that car he gave her towed. He's like the wolf in "Little Red Riding Hood." Beware of men like him. Get out while you're ahead.

This lesson reminds us that Fast Money is not your best friend—

because it prevents you from playing the long game. That's the one where you win a better, bigger, richer life for you and yours.

There are all kinds of legit ways that let you be a dope boy or a dope girl without being a drug dealer—complete with the magnificent lifestyle and the swag of the most successful hustlers but without the risk of getting killed or locked up. There are folks who work legit, respectful jobs who provide services the world needs—teachers, truckers, nurses, doctors, lawyers, engineers, bankers, salespeople, construction or factory workers, and so on. You can have a full-time legit job and build a start-up on the side. There are billionaires with those stories to tell.

Are you down on your luck now? Well, did you know that one of the best times to create a successful start-up is during an economic downturn? That's not luck or the usual pep talk. It's fact.

Don't gamble on your dreams. Do activate the talents and gifts and hidden resources you already have.

CHAPTER 8

MOMMA'S PRAYERS

Keep Track of Your Blessings to Counteract the Curses

Everything you do and everyone in your life is there to teach you something. But sometimes you've got to take the time to reflect in order to appreciate the lessons around you. This was a teaching I wanted to pass on to my kids but whenever I brought it up, asking what they learned at school that day, they would usually respond with, "*Nuthin,*" or "I can't remember." So I gave them the advice, "Why not take notes? Write down what you learned when it happens and then you won't forget."

One of my daughters (they're all super smart) came back with, "Daddy, be truthful, did you always like school?"

"I loved school!" I replied. And that *is* true. "Only I didn't like to study or read or go to class."

All the kids laughed at that. But before long it became a game to them to prove to me that they are learning more than I did when I was young. My oldest two, my sons, even surprised me. I wasn't sure they were college material. Now I'm banking on it.

Whatever is learned is never wasted—so much so it's a blessing. That's why I shifted into calling whatever I had learned "the blessing for the day."

And this is how I introduced my kids to *keeping track of your blessings to counteract the curses*. This lesson is deeper than it may seem. When I refer to curses, I'm talking about those negative forces in our lives that we often can't control—poverty, racism, unhappiness about how we are living and can't escape. I'm also talking about actual curses—when other people's meanness or ignorance is meant to hurt us. When we focus on our blessings instead of our misfortunes, we lift the feeling of being cursed.

Of course, I didn't make up this principle. Throughout the Bible there are numerous reminders to "count your blessings." Not just to count them but to keep track of them by writing them down.

When you write something down, you give it energy in your life. Writing down your blessings is powerful. Seems like we all focus on the bad much more than the good and before long it's a pattern. The more you focus on, talk about, and cry about the bad, the more you feel bad. I'm not saying that you should hold the bad inside and not talk about it. I'm not saying that everything terrible, unfair, and painful that happens should be called "good." I'm not saying you should accept the curses as God's will. I don't believe that. I believe we are all His children, that He is well pleased with us and He wants us to thrive. If we focus on that and keep track of the blessings He sends, we give the good in our lives enough power to counteract the curses.

In the process, this lesson can reveal the ways we sometimes block our own good with attitudes of blame, resentment, judgment, and the withholding of forgiveness. Those are some heavy burdens. Not much feels better or more freeing than to just let your unforgiveness go. Yep, I know, it's hard to do.

My story of learning to battle the curses proves that.

Divine Intervention

From the time my momma died after I had just turned eleven, I accepted that the blessings sent my way came from her prayers—both in this life and from up above. With the start of those Social Security death benefit checks, I never felt poor again. It's terrible that you should have to lose someone you love to counteract a curse of poverty. But it was her way, I believed, in blessing me with some help. And there were other ways she intervened in my life and let her presence be known. Sometimes I could feel her so strongly I'd imagine her pulling strings from on high when a bit of divine intervention was most needed.

Was that Momma whispering in my ear, telling me to use my words and have the nerve to make Judge Turner and everybody in the courtroom laugh? Could she have been reminding me of all those years I was so mouthy as a child, and suggesting that this might be a time to put that skill to use?

Which brings me back to where I started telling y'all my story and how Judge Turner pounded the gavel in the middle of all that laughter before giving me the sentence of ten years of probation instead of jail time.

The look on my face after being told I was free to go must have prompted Judy Rocker, the fine-looking, black-haired, older white woman assigned as my probation officer, to come over and repeat everything my lawyer had just told me.

For once in my life, I was at a loss for words.

Judy shook her head, like she, too, believed Judge Turner's sentence was miraculous. As I turned to walk out, she handed me her card and pointed to where her office was down the hall on the first floor, and said, "Call me next week so we can set up a meeting."

Of all the angels and positive influences Momma sent to help me, Judy Rocker wasn't exactly who you'd expect. At first, we didn't seem to have a lot in common. But she was from Millen, too, and the white version of Kountry. She loved God, read the Bible, and was a lifelong follower of Jesus. So maybe there was some logic in how I began to trust her, and, before long, how I got comfortable talking to her about the traumas of my past.

Looking back, I can see how Judy Rocker became sort of a therapist to me. Lemme tell you, I know a lot of Kountry folk think therapy is just for crazy people. Not me. I think it can be a blessing.

Judy probably saw herself as a mother figure, I guess, except . . . I had a *huge* crush on her. Didn't matter to me that she was white, married, and fifty years old, and I was twenty and had two kids.

At one point, I even wanted to marry Judy Rocker. That *was* crazy. I know. We came from different sides of the railroad tracks, not to mention that her husband had been my Little League coach, years earlier. He was a good guy and a great father to their children, and I wasn't about to break them up. Still, because Judy and I could talk about everything and anything, we had a deep and soulful connection.

Judy wasn't a racist, but she probably was raised as one. This was the first time I'd ever talked to a white person directly about prejudice and white stereotypes held of Black people—which meant I got to hear a perspective I'd never heard before and then I could talk about my experiences of racism, providing a perspective she'd never heard. She was the one who admitted that she probably wouldn't let me date her daughter—not because I wasn't white but because I wasn't rich.

I was kind of insulted. But you know what? If it was my daughter, at that time, I would have preferred that she went out with someone rich, too, as opposed to Dewayne Colley. Then again, I wasn't who I was gonna be yet.

Judy and I could argue about why it was wrong to generalize about people, Black or white. And it could get heated. We could throw verbal bricks at each other, but we kept it free-flowing and safe. Like a college sociology class!

We talked about the unfairness of the justice system. Even if the police were more vicious in Atlanta, white judges in the Kountry were ten times as harsh. My cousin in Atlanta had gotten one year of probation for the same crime that I'd gotten ten years of probation for. White defendants got slaps on their wrists and clean records, no matter where they lived.

Judy listened and mostly agreed that the system was unfair.

One of the many things I admire about women is how most of them pay attention to details. Judy had that habit down—how she dressed all put together, in styles that looked expensive (but weren't) and how she was always thoughtful about matching her lipstick to her accessories and the way she fixed her hair just right.

We always talked much longer than our officially scheduled one-hour appointments. I might arrive at Judy's office at the courthouse in the afternoon and I'd stay until it was dark outside. A lot of times, the security guards would come around, acting nosy, with the excuse that they were locking up the building.

Judy always reassured them that she'd let us out and lock up. Then we'd keep talking, sometimes until late at night. The guards musta thought I needed serious reforming—and that was true.

By the time I did leave and speed the five minutes home to the apartment I'd gotten and where I stayed with Queet and our kids, *oooooh*, she would be waiting up for me, arms folded and eyes squinted—mad!

"Wayne!" She'd give me that universal hands-up-in-the-air gesture for "*Where you been!?*" Eventually, Queet came right out and asked, "You messin' around with Judy Rocker? Somethin' goin' on?"

Offended, I shrugged her off, saying something like, "Girl, you crazy?"

Nuthin was goin' on other than the thrill of getting to talk to someone I respected about the future. In Millen, Georgia, of all places. Not your everyday conversation. We talked about more than just paying bills and meeting obligations. Judy even once confided that her dream was to retire from being a probation officer and become a wedding planner.

That was startling. Nobody I knew ever talked about working a regular nine-to-five job to support themselves and their family—while also having a bigger dream on the side or in front of them that they were working toward.

Her openness got me to talking about my rap career—and to thinking that not only could I work legit, keep my commitment to my nine-to-five job on a team with Georgia Power & Electric, but I didn't have to give up my dream of making it big as a rapper. As I looked back, my love of words and rhyming had been with me since childhood and I'd never given up on myself. Clearly, the plan to become a PE teacher went by the wayside, but it was never my life's ambition. Really, it was just a means to an end to afford to get into music. In fact, I was more married to the rap game than to any other ambition. My freestylin was still in the moment but lyrically my writing was getting more into storytelling. I even recorded a song with an R & B track and me rapping over it, "Oh Momma," and I put the question out there: *"Momma, I miss you. Why'd you have to go and die when I was just eleven? The only thing I can hope is that you went to heaven. . . ."*

The time had come to start making moves. So I used some of the money left over from my tax return and paid to go into a studio. The last time I'd invested in my career was back in high school with my first CD single. It wasn't bad. But this time my production values improved a lot and the song concept was *poppin'*!

The lyrics had come out of me freestylin about how I could still have a magnificent lifestyle and work legit. *"You ain't gotta be a dope boy to have money"* was the lead-in lyric, a phrase I'd heard before but never really believed so much until now. And I went on about how me and my Working Man partners could roll into the club without the big fake hundreds. The ad-lib was "every Thursday," because I was getting paid once a week on Thursdays. And having peace of mind.

Then I took aim for real—in the song and when I was out and about—talking trash about the dope boys still in the streets. Now that I wasn't selling drugs, I gave them a hard time. "Y'all still out here hustling? I got me a nine-to-five job." My flex was more golden than a Rolex.

I even wore my Georgia Power & Electric hat in the picture I put on the CD cover. Judy Rocker was impressed. She saw that I was serious.

Now, Judy Rocker was not a hip-hop lover or expert. And she didn't know much about the music business. But she assumed, like many people, that rappers only come from the City and can't really be Kountry.

Naw, I told her, it may be more uncommon in little towns, but playing with words and beats is as true to the Kountry as anywhere. Like David in the Bible, watching his sheep and making up Psalms. Rap was in me, something I'd always liked doing—and I freestyled for her right there in the courthouse. In hindsight, it was hilarious. I made up a bar or two on the spot, all about looking into a woman's eyes and seeing if her heart was true. "*I played chess in the life. She was the queen, I was the rook . . . and broke the rules before we got shook.*"

Judy became a believer.

In a comedy video, years later, I borrowed from my experience with Judy but turned it around. Drip's probation officer pops up on him in the streets to see if he's working a legit job and he tells her, yes, he's in the music business—Drip Entertainment. Instead of backing another artist, Drip's got someone even better—himself. Ms. Johnson doesn't believe he can really rap. She makes the mistake of laughing at him. Drip, mad, tells her, "You just a probation officer. You not my audience. Don't laugh. I'll buy you an office for where you can go stay so you won't be poppin' up in these streets." The thing about Drip is, he can be funny, how he talks and dresses and thinks, but do *not* make fun of his dreams.

Judy Rocker would never have laughed at me. And I never took her belief in me for granted.

On the other hand, as the Man in the City, in and around Millen, I realized that most people wouldn't take me as seriously if I was just a guy who worked at Georgia Power & Electric. But if they knew I was a legit Working Man *and* a rapper, I could keep my credibility in the streets without dealing drugs.

The record became a modest local hit. But, no surprise, the usual obstacle was in the way. Without the funding to afford a promoter, my CD could only take me so far. Soon the temptation to go after some Fast Money crept in, sorry to say. But I held strong. For a time, I even convinced myself that maybe I was being too biggidy and why not settle into the Kountry rhythm? The simple, back-to-basics life for me and my family didn't have to be so bad. The thought of having a small house with a yard and a lawn mower—the kind you ride around like a cowboy—was sort of appealing.

Besides, I really liked my job. I was blessed to be employed during such hard economic times—with all the major plants in Millen shutting down. Contracting for Georgia Power & Electric was an answered prayer. I liked getting up and going to work every day. Putting on work clothes and heavy gloves. Driving a big truck, traveling around the state, cleaning up spills that were typically caused by oil-filled transformers that had fallen, and learning how the business was run.

Believe it or not, if you look at my company today, how I run it, I can point you to the lessons learned from Georgia Power. The principles are the same for any contractor that is employed by a large corporation.

In the beginning, members of my work crew referred to me as "Double Aught." Sounded cool. Like James Bond. Like Secret Agent 007. It was cool until I found out that Double Aught (or Double Zero) was my name 'cause I knew *nuthin* at the start. They understood that I'd been hired without any experience off the strength of a recommendation. The jury was out. Either I was going to be a danger to the team or an asset. That would depend on how much and how fast I could learn.

So, just like at MI, when I had to prove myself by feeding glass into a machine faster and more efficiently than anyone else, the same was true at Georgia Power.

The job was dangerous. The more experienced coworkers warned me about getting electrocuted.

"Electrocuted?" I asked the first time it was pointed out to me what not to touch.

My supervisor gave me a look like I was not hearing him. "I said, 'Don't touch none of this, because these'll electrocute you.'"

Hmmmm. I pointed, "That one little screw?" I took my hand to touch it slightly to show him the one I meant and—ZZZZZZZZZT! The electric buzz traveled through my body, much to my *shock*. I don't know how I did it, but aside from my eyes bugging, I covered up how bad the jolt was. Nobody realized I'd just about fried my hair. After that, I never repeated the same mistake of almost blowing myself up.

It wasn't long before I started to pay attention to company policies and to understand smart business management, especially how to motivate workers on the job. Georgia Power took care of their employees. Some corporations, big or small, try to cut costs on the backs of their workers. What happens next is that those workers will go somewhere else and cost the business more to have to hire and train new people. Whenever I got my Thursday paycheck, I remember being surprised to see that I'd been paid for the whole week, even if our team didn't have work calls on one of the days. If we finished a job in less time than it normally took, we still got paid for the time we were supposed to have been on the clock. Salary structures can benefit both workers and employers.

I didn't know how much I absorbed on the job until much later— when I built a production team that included my brothers. Days can go by without work. But everybody still gets paid. That's not family pay. It's company rules. When we are on the move, we have long, hard hours and the salary covers it. But I believe that employees—human resources—are the top assets in any company.

At the same time, I learned that if workers weren't pulling their weight while on the job for Georgia Power, *bam*, they were gone. That's why I'm careful about who I hire—because I don't like to let people go. But if there's one thing I learned, both in the streets and as a nine-to-five Working Man, it's that if you are the boss, you gotta have thick skin and get rid of weak links.

The other business skill I learned in my time at Georgia Power was the importance of keeping up with paperwork, time sheets, customer orders, invoices, you name it. Plus, I gained an added appreciation for filing taxes and what was involved.

Things were going so good for me on the straight and narrow that when Pops got out of prison after serving three-and-a-half years on a drug-trafficking charge, he was inspired to give up hustling. Instead, he started hustling in legit ways—with a newspaper route and cutting grass, all that. Whatever he could find to do.

During these years, there was a shift in my relationship with my daddy. The truth remains the truth—he wasn't there for me during the years when I most needed and wanted a father. But Momma's prayers had sent me the help of Momma Doog and my cousin Jack. Plus, in the absence of a father figure, I learned to look to myself. So I forgave Pops and tried to be there for him, because, in the end, withholding forgiveness would have been toxic to me. Or maybe I realized the ability to forgive my daddy was something Momma would have wanted me to have.

All I know is that when I turned twenty-one, I promised myself that if I could bless anyone in my family or anyone my eyes could see or anyone my hands could touch, I would do it—because I could.

The Blessing Book

Toward the end of 2009, with my twenty-second birthday coming up fast, I confided in Judy Rocker about the curse of addiction that had gotten both my parents at that age. She was wise enough to observe that addiction wasn't my real fear.

What was it? I gave the question a lot of thought.

My fear was giving in or giving up on my vision for the future and not following through on everything I'd promised myself that I would. The dread of spinning my wheels and getting stuck ate at me. I had to get out if I wanted to push my music. Queet and I talked about breaking up. I'd keep my job, and, of course, support her and our (now three) kids—Tony, Temar, and Malia. My daughter had arrived in this world premature but with a spiritual knowingness in her eyes that caught you off guard. She was smart, strong, and, in time, had a lot to say. Like a prophet.

By this point, our two-bedroom apartment was busting at the seams. Not just with me, my baby mama, a preschooler, a toddler, and an infant, but also with more of Queet's family members. The bills that I was expected to pay kept piling up. Finally, one day when I was driving to go help bail out another one of her family members at the jail, I said something to Queet's momma about maybe they could help out with some of the bills if they were living there.

Oooooh, she didn't like that. Talkin' real fast, she snapped and said,

"You better stop complainin' about the bills, because we can come back and take out child support on you and your life 'bout to be over!"

What? Nobody had to force me to do what I already was doing. I didn't like being threatened that they'd even try to use the system against me.

"You'll be fine," Judy said when I told her how much that threat stressed me out. "You've always taken care of your responsibilities and you love your kids." She was 100 percent confident I'd solve the problem. "You're a prodigy," Judy told me then. "You won't let the child support system outsmart you."

I didn't know what a prodigy was, but it sounded like a compliment. "Thank you . . . I guess."

Judy went on. "I've never seen anyone like you. You were born with something special. You can get your way out of anything. I'd put my money on you any day."

I held on to those words and brought them to mind whenever I faced other, bigger challenges.

Exchanges like that one helped me look at the things I called "curses" and start to see them in a different light. Ironically, as I now understood, I wasn't as afraid of the curse of addiction as I was of never giving my destiny a chance. Then it hit my spirit that we all have addictions, but it's up to us to keep the self-destructive ones in check. How?

At our next meeting, I'll never forget, Judy starts the appointment by handing me a book. "I got this for you," she says.

"Thank you," I say, surprised. Then I open it and see the pages are all blank.

Judy explains that she is giving me a blank book so that I can keep track of my blessings. "It's not a diary for writing down everything that's going on," she told me. "Or to complain. It's not a cursing book.

It's more for writing down the good things that God did for you today and that you can be thankful for."

I called it my "blessing book."

That blank book, which I kept and wrote in every day from then on, changed my life. Eventually, I had to go out and get another book to write in. From day one, every entry has been short and slightly different but always starts and ends the same way. I simply start each one by thanking God for waking me up that morning and for putting me in a position to help someone else that day—to be of service somehow.

Ever since the day my momma died, I hadn't been to church hardly at all. Part of that was because it was mostly my momma who had taken me to church and no one else wanted to take me on a regular basis. Momma had always taught me that you didn't need to go to a place of worship to have a connection to God. So I was my own church, processing my own understanding of right and wrong, and living a life that was more spiritual than religious.

One of the reasons I really liked talking to Judy Rocker was that she had a deep knowledge of the Bible and could cite the stories and verses that supported a point she was trying to make.

By writing down the blessings I've received and the ones I've given, I've tallied that many more in total—and this leaves less room for the curses.

The blessing book has also kept me honest and accountable to myself.

My twenty-second birthday came and went. The family curse had no power over me. I didn't suddenly decide to get high and become an addict to drugs or alcohol. Fending off other addictions was a work in progress. Lust, in particular.

Call me a slow learner in some areas. Like I said before, relying on luck does *not* work as contraception. Well, that's a short version of how, during this time period, two more beautiful baby daughters of mine were born to two different women who were not Queet. This coincidence was something that I didn't know about for a long time. That's three baby mamas and five children—including my lovely daughter Alayah, poised and cool from the start, and my miracle child, Christiana (who I didn't know about until later).

If ever there was a time when I could have used some Fast Money, it was at age twenty-two—right as I was moving out from Queet and starting to see Keisha, baby mama of my next daughter, Zarhia, who turned out to have an outgoing, social personality. Keisha, not from Millen originally but who stayed there with family, was part–Puerto Rican/part-Black, beautiful, and supportive. She was always easygoing—unless something set her off.

Meanwhile, it didn't take a math genius to see I had more overhead than income. Something had to change. For more than two years and a couple of months, I'd been a model citizen. My determination to stay legit was *rock solid*. My job at Georgia Power was high on the blessing list. Even higher was the judge's leniency. My momma's prayers had been answered and I had faith they would continue to bless me.

Then reality tapped me on the shoulder one day. After cashing my check, taking care of baby mamas, some of their relatives, and our kids, plus some "looking out" payments for my family members (you gotta look out for the ones you love) and some additional bills, I had sixty dollars left to my name. It was déjà vu all over again.

Riding in the car with my daddy on our way to my grandmomma Mary's house for a party thrown by my sisters, I did something I'd sworn never to do and asked him, "Pops, you got forty dollars I can borrow?" One hundred dollars would let me eat for the rest of the week and put gas in my car.

"Son, I was 'bout to ask you the same thing."

That was *it*. I had to find a way to beat the system for all of us. I didn't know how but knew we needed money fast. With that thought, I made a plan to visit a bank in Swainsboro the very next day—to ask for a loan. Eventually, I would use that money to get back into hustling, even though that wasn't my first idea at all.

Daddy flashed me a skeptical glance. All he ever knew was the dope game—since before I was born. He muttered something, half-joking, like, "You fixin' to rob a bank?"

I laughed. I didn't have it all laid out yet, but I'd borrowed money for my car before and knew it could be done.

Keep Track of Your Blessings for a Rainy Day

One of the reasons I want to share some of the less flattering parts of my story is to encourage anyone and everyone to know that your blessings won't be blocked if you haven't always made perfect choices. Not all my choices were good ones, as you can see. But the fact that I chose to keep a connection to my momma was one that gave my life purpose at every step.

Whatever you believe, I hope you know that somewhere there is someone—alive or not—whose prayers for you are being answered to give you blessings every day. You are alive and reading these words, for one thing. You have brought yourself this far so at the least you have blessed yourself.

Buddy actually understands this principle. His take: "Hey, little dahlin', I give away money so I can keep my blessings." Drip is also a natural when it comes to appreciating what he has. He's the first to say, "Yuh, I count my blessings like I count my money. Every day!"

If you want to counteract curses, why not try getting yourself your own blessing book? Give it a shot and see if you don't find the negatives in your life begin to fall away the more you keep track of the ways you have been blessed. Whether it is just that you woke up today in your right mind or that you were put in a position to bless someone else, it all is worth counting.

If you have been blessed in money or material things, by all means you can write those things down. But I like the point in the quote by the Roman emperor Marcus Aurelius who said it best:

> *Don't set your mind on things you don't possess as if they were*
> *yours, but count the blessings you actually possess and think how*
> *much you would desire them if they weren't already yours. But*
> *watch yourself, that you don't value these things to the point of*
> *being troubled if you should lose them.*

Keeping track of your blessings is not just about paying attention to all the good you have. It's also about reminding yourself that you are always worth that good.

PART II

CHAPTER 9

GETTIN' PAPER

Mind Your Business

Growing up in the Kountry, I learned early in life that everything has its season. There is a season when you are learning the basics of what life's got to teach you and there is a season when it's time to put those lessons to use—when you may still stumble and fall before you get it right.

Mind your business was something I first learned by watching my daddy and uncle at work as different kinds of hustlers. Each of them had their own ways of minding their business with thought and focus, but also of *not* minding their business. The most common way of not minding your business is simply when you slack off or get distracted. At times, Pops could be the most serious, focused, and talented at what he did. Unfortunately, he was also easily distracted. Usually by women. Or by dipping into his own supply.

In all fields, there are multiple ways of minding your business—or failing to do so. If you are starting a company, minding your business requires you to pay attention to every detail, and to all the different phases of the operation. You might hire people who are good at what they do to take over some of the tasks that you don't have time to do. That's called delegating. I'm all for it. But you've still got to pay attention to how anyone who works for you or with you is able to focus—or not. Pay attention to whether or not they're helping to improve your overall bottom line.

If you are working for someone else, learning to mind your business is a great lesson for advancing up the ladder. People worry all the time about how so-and-so got a promotion when you didn't. Maybe it was unfair. But lemme tell you something—if you spend your time complaining about the system being designed to keep you back, you'll overlook the fact that the best way to beat the system is to mind *your* business. Or worse, you can get distracted or caught up in the gossip. Or you can decide you could do someone else's job better. I say, that's spreading your energy thin. Why clutter your brain?

Mind your business.

One of the best ways to keep your mind on your business and your business on your mind is to be clear about your motivation. There is *nuthin* wrong with deciding that making paper is your priority. That drove me and was something I was absolutely meant to do, whatever it was gonna take. At the same time, minding my business also taught me that making paper shouldn't be the ultimate goal. It's what makes the ultimate goal possible.

Walt Disney once said, "We don't make movies to make money, we make money to make more movies." He set the stage for family entertainment on a level that has never been reached by any other show business entity.

In other words, getting that paper has never been my end goal; it's just a means of creating opportunities to do the work I love and make the life I want for me and mine. Minding your business teaches you how to put that principle into action.

I wasn't eager to step back into hustling. I couldn't make the same mistakes and think I'd get lucky this time. Good thing that I'd learned that earlier lesson. Instead, I would have to mind my business better than before—in a new way. That brought out a new side of me— a side that would definitely come in handy later on in the legit world.

Always remember—lessons learned in the dark are just as effective when used in the light.

The Kountry Art of Persuasion

During the time that my daddy was locked up, he spent a lot of hours in the prison library reading books on prosperity and on spiritual laws for success. Every time he finished a book, he'd send me a recommendation that I check it out for myself. That's how I began to read more and think more about why it's important to mind your business. Robert Greene's books *The 48 Laws of Power* and *The Art of Seduction* spoke to me. When Pops came home, and we were enjoying living and working legit, we'd sit and talk about the concepts in the different books over games of checkers. We never talked about going back to hustling because we'd moved on for good, as far as we were both concerned.

So on that day in early 2010 when we went to Swainsboro to get a bank loan, I was unsure what our next move was supposed to be. I knew hard work was key to minding your business. But I also had read that it's better to work smart than just to work hard. If you really want to make some money, the books all said, one smart way is to use somebody else's money to fund your dream.

Pops came with me to my bank meeting with a nice dude by the name of Affy—one of those Kountry names that you could spend an hour talking about.

We talked family, kids, weather, and my job at Georgia Power. My first mention of getting a loan was that my Crown Victoria needed work.

"How much you think?" Affy asked.

"Five thousand," I began and explained, "it's an old car and everything's 'bout to go at once. But it's what gets me to my job every day."

Affy thought the 5k was steep. My Ronald McDonald–looking, yellow and red Crown Victoria wasn't worth more than $1,500 at this point, which meant the title wasn't much to put up for collateral. Affy looked through his files and saw that I'd gotten a loan before for car repairs and had paid it back. "Maybe I could do about half of what you're asking for," he offered.

I understood, I told him. And then, as if I was telling him something confidential, I added, something along the lines of, "You know, I'm fixin' to take off as a rapper. I got a CD out and they love it around here and in Millen. I was thinking of building my own studio, you feel me?"

Affy was intrigued. "You go by Dewayne Colley as a rapper?"

"Nah, I go by Kountry Wayne."

Affy thought it over and then said, "Yeah, it has a ring to it." But he still wasn't convinced.

Then I threw in the fact that I could expect a raise later in the year and I really needed to get some bills paid off, maybe move to a bigger place.

In the Kountry, everyone relates to the subject of family responsibilities. Affy decided he could crunch the numbers and make the loan work.

You'll notice that I was just speaking truth. No bull. No hype. Truth is essential for the art of persuasion. Some people abuse that tactic by telling a heap of lies with a dose of the truth. Everything I said was the truth—even if I didn't say everything. My way of convincing him that I was a good investment was just being real.

Affy escorted us out to the teller's window and shook my father's hand and then mine.

Pops, his eyes wide with disbelief, waited nearby in the bank lobby, watching as I cashed the loan check there and then.

We walked out to my car as he said under his breath, "Yeah, son, I was right! We did jes rob a bank!"

Gotta admit, I was surprised at the power of just being friendly and having charisma. Robert Greene wrote about the trait of being charismatic—a word I didn't normally use before that. Wow.

Without being able to communicate my realization yet, I started to appreciate, from then on, how we are all given certain natural gifts that can be monetized. Of course, the word *monetize* wasn't how folks talked in those days. It just hit me that our natural gifts are given to us so we can enrich ourselves. Swag was something we all understood as being like honey to bees. Charisma is not that different from swag.

So, when you mind your business, you learn how to maximize a resource that is free to you already—like charisma. You can't push it too far, but just be yourself. To test out my theory, not too many months later I went to a second bank around the corner and helped Pops fill out another loan for the same amount. We put the *h-u-s-t-l-e* in hus-tlers. All I had to do was agree to cosign it. My credit score wasn't great but it was better than his.

When I got the first loan, I still believed a legit side hustle was pos-sible. In fact, when I took home that first $5,000, I had the discipline to pay bills, repair the car, and take care of baby mamas and kids and make sure my daddy Skip and I had some peace-of-mind money in our pockets. That's how I managed to burn through $2,000 in a matter of days.

Not trusting myself, I asked Pops to hold on to the remaining $3,000. Otherwise, I was sure to go through it way too fast.

Within a week, I'd gone back to thinking about the one business I really knew. I came up with a short-term plan. When I went to talk to my daddy about it, he was already on the same page, telling me, "I was 'bout to surprise you." Then he went on to say he had a connect out of state ready to get us started.

Pops and I would be working together this time. Being on proba-tion meant I really couldn't get arrested for even the suspicion of being back in the game or I'd be going straight to jail. It made sense that my father, who had already served his time for his last charge, would take on more of the risk. So we used the $3,000 and jumped back into busi-ness, keeping our roles separate. I would run my own part and had dealers I supplied so my hands were relatively clean. Pops reminded me that this was a means to an end. He put it this way: "We do this for a minute 'til the microphone blow up." He *believed.* He might not have been there for me in my childhood, but he was for me in the streets.

From Monday to Friday, I was a regular Joe Working Man, legit all the way, and a hustler just on weekends. More or less. The streets knew

I was back but if you didn't know, you wouldn't know. Without a hitch, business jumped.

After a couple of months, I stopped telling myself that this was only gonna be a short-term thing. I still believed in the bigger dream that I'd make it in music and would use incoming funds to keep that rolling, but until that day arrived, I was back in the game. I stopped making excuses for makin' paper and makin' moves. But, minding my business, I was quiet, real quiet. Just "shhhhhhhhh."

It took a lot of discipline to avoid an appearance of being a hustler, or, as Drip would say, *not* to look like what I was doing. I gave away as much money as I could do without, partly for my conscience and partly to avoid becoming too attached to the things that money could buy. I had my mind on my busines enough to know that flaunting money was dangerous. My tougher, sterner side started to emerge at times. Usually, I used my humor and my intuition to avoid a battle over turf or any kind of street problems that would result in violence.

With an income stream, in 2010 I started to really push Kountry Wayne—from buying the studio equipment I'd promised myself to getting my name shouted out in the clubs. Every weekend. My reputation as a playa and a rapper began to take off. And now that I wasn't stretched so thin on bills, I could use my paycheck money for promotion and blow it all on purpose.

Clubs were poppin' in those days in every Kountry city and town, every highway and byway all around southeast Georgia—across Screven County due east of Millen, down through my stomping grounds in Statesboro all the way to Savannah (population 146,000). Every payday I'd cash my legit check and ask to have it back in single-dollar bills that I'd take with me to the clubs.

In advance, I'd pay the DJ to announce me and play a hit song to accompany my arrival. The minute the DJ saw me come in, he'd get on the mic, shout out, "Kountry Wayne in the building!" and put on the record. Then I'd come in throwing money.

Mannnnnn, people in the club *loved* it. The DJs would use "*Make It Rain*" (Fat Joe/Lil Wayne) as my theme song and I'd walk in, literally making it rain, throwing green cash money up in the air to rain over the crowd, while I rapped over the beat: "Y'all gotta get yo umbrella ready!"

Word of my club charisma spread, slow for a while, and then with momentum—*Kountry Wayne makes it rain. Yeah, Kountry Wayne be having that money now!*

Whenever I checked in with Judy Rocker, I was able to honestly tell her that my career was moving forward. Of course, the last thing I could admit was that I was hustling again. I'd talk about how great it was working all over the state of Georgia and getting to meet different kinds of people on the job, including a project not far from Atlanta. It was ideal because then I could work during the weekdays but make music at night and on weekends. The equipment I'd bought was housed in a recording studio I'd help build with my cousin Travis. I even started recording with a hip-hop group or, should I say, a duo made up of me and my homie, Devon, who worked with me at Georgia Power. We weren't bad!

The other thing I shared with Judy was that I had finally met the woman I thought was "the one"—who was barely showing any interest in me. That had never happened. Gena—stunning, independent, and ambitious—didn't need or want a man to take care of her and that made me pursue her even harder. I confidently promised Judy that one day I was going to marry Gena and then, well, we'd be looking for a wedding planner.

Everything was going so smoothly, I didn't want to jinx it. So I kept on my toes, even more than usual. Of everything that could go wrong, the one thing that I didn't worry about and knew I could count on was my Slow Money salary job with Georgia Power. Minding my business had taught me that keeping a nine-to-five job was a *must* if I was gonna be quietly hustling again.

Well, I don't care what line of work you are in—legit or not, working for someone else or for yourself—no income stream is guaranteed for good. So you'd better have a plan B. And I was about to find that out.

When the Shoe Drops

The word had come out to the field—to Pensacola, Florida—from the home office of the contracting company, Caddell, one day during lunch. It was July 2010 and the boss of our team mentioned it out of the blue. He didn't say who the employee was, but apparently something had turned up in a background check of somebody on our team.

"I wonder who it is?" said one of the guys. "Hell, if I know," said another.

"I know who it is" is all I said.

Everyone looked at me in disbelief. They loved me. I worked hard, was an asset on the team, and had become known as their free, on-the-job entertainment. Nobody wanted me to go. I shrugged it off, not saying anything else.

That night the top supervisor, Carl, took me out to dinner.

Apparently, the contract with Georgia Power was up and Caddell was switching to another electric utility. Routine background checks were par for the course whenever a new contract was being signed. When I was first hired, my indictment in Millen hadn't come in, so my record was felony-free at the time. Two-and-a-half years later, my record obviously had been updated. The shoe had dropped, after all this time.

For most of the day I'd managed to stay up and accept my fate. But faced with the reality of the system, I felt down. How could they cut me loose because of something in the past? Hadn't I proven myself for over two-and-a-half years? It hit me hard as I faced the truth that I really didn't want to go back to the streets 100 percent.

But there was no negotiating with the powers that be. It was a big reminder of the lesson learned earlier that your rep is everything, good or bad.

Within a few days, I heard from the main office and they offered me another job on a contract that wasn't going to run out for another two years. They were trying to help by giving me time to get my record clear.

Before taking the offer, I decided to think it over. My judgment was clouded by the feeling of being mad at the system. For some months I'd been hustling on the side quietly, so it wasn't like my conscience was spotless. It just always seemed like the deck was stacked. So I called back and said, "I appreciate y'all giving me the opportunity and letting me work up until now," and then turned down the offer.

On the drive back from Florida, I questioned my decision. I thought about the fact that not having a full-time day job would free me up to spend more time with my kids. The joy of being with them put everything else in perspective. In my business dealings as a hustler, by now

I'd really found a Drip side of me—laid-back Kountry on the one hand but all business on the other. I trusted almost no one outside of my family. There was no room for error that could lead to my being caught and having to serve time. None. I wasn't playing.

The thought occurred to me: *If only there was a solution for a legit job that would let me make the kind of money I was able to make hustling, then I could be out of the streets for good.* I flashed on my daddy's promise that we'd only hustle until the mic blew up, which reassured me. But what was it gonna take? The answer that came back to me was a promotional plan to get my name out! But everybody was doing the same thing, basically paying for radio play and exposure that way. My angle had to be so fresh it would help put Kountry Wayne on the map of southeast Georgia like nobody's business.

Then another shoe dropped. The good shoe. My idea was so fresh I called my sister Torrie from the car that I was gonna come and see her the next day at work and tell her my idea.

CUT TO: The next day, a humid and hot afternoon in Statesboro. My sis Torrie is at the Walmart gas station where she works and spots my Crown Vic in the parking lot. She hurries over. I jump out and meet her.

Torrie: (laughing) *For somebody out of a nine-to-five job, you look a little too happy, bro. What you need to tell me that can't wait?*
Me: (unable to contain my excitement) *Hey, sis, I need you to help me get a group of girls together to be part of Kountry Wayne Entertainment. I need four or five of the most beautiful girls in the City. I'ma have 'em dress up nice to come out to the clubs with me. And I need your help.*

155

Torrie: *I'm in!*

Me: *You'll be one of the girls but I need you to manage the group.*

Torrie: (thinking) *Cool. Got you, bro.*

Me: *Boy, I'm 'bout to take over the streets! I need y'all to stay fresh. I'm gonna pay to keep y'all's hair done, your nails, lashes, wigs, and everything. We need different colors of wigs, too. Red, blue, purple, green. We'll do a photo shoot. And we should get T-shirts with the group name on it. Hey, and maybe y'all could have a song, a record.*

Torrie: *What you gonna call the group?*

Me: (looking up at her, taking a beat) *Exotic.*

Torrie: *Exotic? That's pretty good.*

Neither one of us realized that my idea for the Exotic Girls was much more than just a plan to get me hot. It was actually the first half of a plan that would change me from street hustler to serious entrepreneur. Better still, it was going to create a legit opportunity for a lot of other people. More than anything, my brainstorm was about to be proof of the power of great ideas to change your circumstances—almost overnight.

Identify Your Key Distractions

The lesson of why it always matters to mind your business is one I continue to appreciate. There are so many ways you can apply this lesson. Start by identifying some of your key distractions. Is your mind clear? When your mind is clear, you can tap into the spirit of innovation that lives inside of you, ready to deliver ideas when you most need them. If you don't think as clearly as you would like, you might consider cutting back on the habits that keep you from bringing your sharpest and smartest assets to your chosen goals.

I'm not just talking about drinking or getting high, I also mean anything that you consume that might dull your mind. I'm talking about what you feed your spirit as well as your body and your mind. It's the books you read, the content you watch online and on TV, the music you play, the stories you follow. It's the time you spend outside in nature or in mediation and prayer. What if you've got an incredible business idea simmering on the back burner of your brain but the stove top is too crowded for you to get to it? Well, my advice is to get rid of old stuff you've been feeding yourself and find out what can really sizzle in your spirit.

As Buddy would say, "Ehhhh, if it ain't an asset, you need to set it aside, like Buddy always does." Drip's advice is on point: "Don't let *nuthin* extract you from yo dream."

When you start to mind your business, you may also have to look at the friends and family who create unneeded drama in your life. You don't have to cut them out of your life completely. Still, you might ask yourself what they are adding to your life's good and how you are adding to their good.

CHAPTER 10

WOMEN ARE MY STRENGTH

Give Money and Love Unconditionally

Lemme tell you something they don't put in many of the business books I've read or in many books offering spiritual laws for success: the simple fact that love—of every kind—is the greatest, most powerful accelerant and the number one most effective lubricant for the engine of your success.

You might be thinkin', *Wayne, c'mon, there's a lot of poor, unsuccessful people out here who still have love. You sure love's all you're cracking it up to be?*

You've got a point. The problem is that the love power I'm talkin' 'bout comes in how you give it, not how you hope to get it. We all want to be loved in return, of course. But I've learned that the love that most enriches you is the kind you give without any expectation of getting it back or of making any return on the dollar of pure giving.

The more you learn to practice *giving money and love unconditionally,* the faster you can change your mindset about what it means to be rich. Once your mindset changes, well, before long so does your reality.

What you give without condition of being paid in return does come back to you. Call it Karma or God or the Universe, but that is a timeless truth. It doesn't always come back in the form that you expected. True. But most often it comes back many times more than what you originally gave.

For many years I didn't realize that I felt motivated to give to women, in particular, because of the things I was never able to give to my momma. Some of the women reminded me of my mother, you might say. But mostly I didn't want them to have to struggle without someone looking out. I didn't want them to have to go looking for sugar daddies like Buddy, something I saw growing up. I hated for any man to raise a hand to a woman or to talk about them with disrespect.

In my early days of rapping, I'd throw out a word or two, like *bitches* or *ho.* But then I had kids and they had mamas, so I quit that fast.

Later, in my comedy, I added a bit about why I can't call a woman a ho—because I have eight daughters and the law of averages tells me there's gonna be one in the bunch. Well? And I know which one it is. (Just kidding.)

A lot of people might think that women are my weakness. It's the opposite. Women have always been my strength. If you are a woman or if you love a woman, you've been given the keys to the kingdom. The unconditional, devoted love you have to give to a woman—or, alright, to lots of women—can absolutely lubricate and accelerate your success.

Women to me are the mothers of invention, imagination, and inspiration. Every breakthrough big-money idea that ever came to me was because of a woman. I wouldn't have even known about social media if it wasn't for my sister Shavonne, who told me if I really wanted to introduce myself to Gena (who was from Statesboro), I should get on the Internet and join Facebook. I didn't get it. But I certainly would in time.

Many of the women I know don't even realize what powers they have and what queens they really are. If a man or a woman hasn't given you some unconditional love *and* money, give it to yourself. If you are a woman who isn't getting the love you deserve from your special someone, you can always move on. It's hard to walk away, but, if you aren't being seen for who you are, walk away. You know why? Because no one really sees you until you are walking away from them. Go give your good love to someone who's got some for you. It's like gum that gets stuck on you. You need some other gum to get that stuck gum off you. Find someone else to love and enjoy.

The lesson of giving money and love unconditionally has applications when it comes to business. When I first went into show business, I would walk into meetings with agents and managers and producers thinking that they had the power to approve of me or reject me. That was hit-and-miss. It made me have to grovel. Not my style. So I changed my approach. Instead of thinking they had something I wanted, my idea was that I had something they wanted. I stopped being intimidated. My attitude was that they should be happy to meet me because I was about to make them some money. Strong women taught me that. Eventually, I became so confident it was like, *These people are lucky to meet me!* I feel that way in front of audiences. If my intention is to entertain, why not give love and the value of my company for the next hour or so?

There is always room for more love, even with a business connection.

Taking that a step further, when you have a brainstorm for a business that can benefit you and lots of other people—maybe even helping them create businesses of their own—that's a form of money and love that you give unconditionally. You can lift whole economies that way.

I've had some of those brainstorms—the kind that really make it rain. All thanks to women in my life.

Time to Turn It Up

Breakthrough business ideas can hit you in the least likely places. An idea I never saw coming just about struck me like lightning one night as I was waiting in line to get into a place called the Legion in Screven County—the club where I first started to throw money on the weekends. Screven County, due east of Jenkins County, where Millen is, borders South Carolina on the other side. Screven is so rural—just a handful of tiny towns—that the Legion was basically stuck out in the Kountry, one of only two nightspots for Black club goers for miles around. The location was great but otherwise, if I had my preference, I'd probably go to Screven's other club, the Spaceship Lounge. *Except* . . . now that I no longer worked for Georgia Power, my job was showing up at all the clubs. The more I connected to fans in the tiny towns and in the bigger ones, the closer that would get me to a lasting, loyal fan base.

Didn't seem to matter that I was getting love in the streets. At the Legion I still had to wait in line to get into the club. Made no sense. Whenever the guys working the door looked out to see how long the line was, if they saw pretty girls waiting, they'd come and get them, or wave them up to the front and on inside. Any men outside in the line had to keep waiting.

Standing there in line I got to thinking hard about a conversation I'd had with Queet after I called her with the news about Georgia Power. Queet was always honest with me and, even if I felt bad hearing a criticism from her, in the end I valued that honesty. She wasn't complaining about me being a playa or having children by other women, or not being the settling-down kind of guy. Queet and I had been together since we were fourteen. We still had real chemistry. She knew who I was and wasn't going to try to change me. But she did surprise me that day when I mentioned to her that Uncle Cleave was telling everyone I was no different from my daddy—that I wouldn't make it out of Millen.

My uncle must've still been mad I kissed on his girlfriend's feet. Whatever it was, it got back to me that when he heard I wasn't working my nine-to-five anymore, he said something like, "Wayne's a lotta talk. He's already got a bunch of baby mamas, a mess of children, and he will still be in the streets until he's fifty. Rap ain't no music and he ain't no rap star." What he said next was where he crossed the line: "Wayne will never be legit."

Like I told Queet, Uncle Cleave was just making himself feel better by downgrading my potential. Rap music was a legit way to make money, I was good, and the mic was 'bout to blow up.

Queet calmly said, "But you ain't workin' legit now."

Her comment cut right through my defenses. In hindsight, I see that she said it with love but meant it to get my attention. She was right, of course, that I needed to turn it up. The rap game was coming along, but was still going to take time. Meanwhile, I had to make at least some money that was Fast but Legit. What kinda work could that be?

That question struck me at the very same moment that my brain tried to sort out a second question about how I could get the line into the club moving faster. An answer came flying back: *What if I hosted a party at the club myself?*

My first thought was: *That's a lotta work to avoid waiting in line.*

Then again, I could use my popularity from the streets, bring in more patrons, earn a cut of the door and the bar, and it would be legit. I wouldn't have to wait in line, my reputation would grow, plus, I could help the club's business on quieter nights.

In a matter of five minutes, my frustration, mixed with the sting of my baby mama's comment, got me to create a new career path—hosting parties in the club! The cherry on top was the fact that I could use those same parties to play my CDs and freestyle live in the club.

Hmmmm, only one problem: How was I gonna get crowds to turn out to a club when there were so many more males than females coming here? I thought for a half-second and then—*bam*—the solution almost knocked me over. The Exotic Girls! If I hired the girls in my entourage to show up at the clubs and help me host the parties, the guys would definitely come in packs just to see and meet the finest and sweetest ladeeees in southeast Georgia. And if word got out that the most popular, trendsetting young ladeeees—the Exotic Girls—were coming to the club, their fine friends and other girls would wanna come to the club. Clean, wholesome, and *legit!*

Even though nobody had said yes to my plan to host parties, I had to congratulate myself. If this worked out, the Exotic Girls could make money, too. Torrie had already talked to a couple of her friends, who said yes, and Shavonne was in, too. Like I said, women are my strength. This was *on!*

As soon as I got into the Legion that night I went in search of the club's owner, B-wood. This guy was black Black, so much so if he put on a black T-shirt, he'd look naked in the club. No longer alive, B-wood gave me my first shot at party promotion and I will be always grateful, even if we didn't always get along. From what I could see, he was not into growing his business much. He had paper enough and a great location, a club, and a fully stocked bar, not to mention women, whom he seemed to attract.

I was eager to help him improve his numbers. But instead of taking the time to talk to me, B-wood let his manager/sidekick, Juju, hear why a Kountry Wayne–hosted party could be a big draw for the club. I made my case. Juju was cool and willing to give it a try.

That's all I had to hear. That night I couldn't sleep with all these creative entertainment ideas pumping in my brain. At this point, I didn't realize it yet, but I was starting to think like a producer—seeing posters and videos and—Why not—even a tour bus. The Exotic Girls were fixin' to set the streets on fire.

Then it dawned on me: I needed some new material for my next CD. If I'd learned anything from hustling, it's that you can lose even your most loyal clientele if you run out of supply. Right there I started to write down some rhymes that would get tongues wagging in the club. My motivation to come up with some ideas that would play well in the club was sky-high. As a party host, an MC, I had to come ready. It's one thing to jump on the mic for a minute and throw out some rhymes. My job was gonna be as a full-on hype man with an entourage of beauties!

One other thought kept me awake that night: How was I gonna get ahold of Gena and hire her to be part of the Exotic Girls? She was perfect. I'd first spotted Gena at the Spaceship Lounge in Screven County back in April. Ever since, I couldn't get her out of my mind. She was so beautiful and so smart, I wasn't surprised to find out she had a lot of admirers. After I joined Facebook, for the sole purpose of becoming friends, it took me weeks to get a response. Finally, she connected with me on the phone, we talked, and she agreed to go out with me.

On the phone, I wasted no time telling her, "We spose to be together. You can't change destiny." I'm real like that. Besides, Gena was like a female version of me—a single, working mom, a ringleader in her own right who, when she walked into clubs, the seas parted. I went so far as to tell her we could be the "it couple." Like Beyoncé and Jay-Z.

Too much? Gena seemed amused.

We set a time to get together, but when the day arrived, just as I was heading home after running errands, she called to say it wasn't gonna work out. Gena gave me no other reason except, "I gotta go get me some money."

I tried to smooth-talk her with the best of my repertoire. But I was impressed that her priority was providing for her daughter, Taylor, who stayed with Gena's momma. Was she giving me the brush-off? Gena clearly didn't want me to know her financial situation. She was working, taking classes at night school, very focused. She wasn't looking for help, which impressed me even more.

I told her to hit me up anytime and she said she would. After that, I didn't hear anything and lost her number. Then, a couple of months later, I had an excuse to go looking for her and see if she would consider being part of the Exotic Girls.

That thought put a smile on my face and I drifted off to sleep just before daybreak. After only a couple of hours, I woke and was about to call Torrie to tell her about my plan to host a party and introduce the Exotic Girls at the Legion. Before I finished dialing Torrie's number, I saw another call coming in and picked it up.

"Hello?"

"Hey, you know who this is?"

I *fo sho* recognized that buttery voice of hers. "Hey, Gena," I said, trying to be cool but feeling like a schoolboy.

"What's goin' on?"

"*Nuthin*. I'm just sitting here thinkin' about you." That would have been about the corniest thing I could have said. *Except* . . . it was completely true. I was so amazed that I had manifested her phone call, out of nowhere, that I was near speechless.

Before we hung up, though, I'd managed to tell her about the Exotic Girls and the parties I was gonna be throwing. She was open, not promising anything. I figured Torrie would take over and get Gena involved, if she was interested. Before we hung up, we made a plan to get together . . . in a month! She made me wait *again*. When the date rolled around, she didn't cancel. Phew! And wow! August 29 was a night to remember. The wait was worth it. Gena said so herself.

Good thing we didn't rush because I was charging ahead on getting ready for the party at the Legion—recording some new songs and coming up with a strategy for getting the microphone to blow up at the same time the parties were taking off. In August I did a photo shoot with the Exotic Girls that was off the chain!

There was one nerve-racking moment when I got to talking to the photographer that Torrie had found—who was great at what he did. He happened to mention that this was a side hustle for him, not enough for him to leave his day job.

"Yeah, I know how that go," I said. Naturally I asked, "What's your nine-to-five?"

"I'm a GBI officer."

"What?" I almost fainted. He meant the Georgia Bureau of Investigation. I put on the most exaggerated smile ever and nodded. "Oh, so you investigate the people who rob the bank and stuff?"

"Naw," he said, "mostly I investigate drug dealers."

Whatever I said next was along the lines of "Interesting," then changed the subject *fast*. The good news was he was more interested in flirting with one of the Exotic Girls than asking me how I made my living!

As we closed in on the September date of the first party, I heard through the grapevine that a lot of people were planning on being there. I had a good feeling about attendance. But I also knew that it might take time before my new legit moneymaking project would start to earn out. Fortunately, the income from hustling was flowing, enough to support my new side hustle. As committed as I was to giving money and love unconditionally, *mannnnnn*, I admit, my monthly overhead was sure adding up by the day.

Shock Test

On the afternoon of our first party at the Legion, I went by the club to make sure everything was in order. The DJ had come by, too, so we could test the sound system and the mic levels. I was not leaving anything to chance. When I got on the mic to see how it sounded, I realized that a speaker was out. This was a problem.

As the DJ and I are trying to fix it, B-wood comes strolling in, not even bothering to introduce himself. He looks at his watch and at the DJ, like, *Why you here now?*

"Wiring is messed up. Can't get the speaker to work."

"And?"

In short, the DJ says, "If it gets packed in here, we have to push up the volume and then we get distortion."

B-wood rolls his eyes. "Packed? No need to worry about that. It's a slow Friday."

Then I pipe up. "Sheeeit! Hey, you don't know who I am. They comin' here tonight!"

B-wood squints his eyes to get a good look at me. I squint back at him. "We'll see," he says and leaves us to get the speaker fixed.

For the next several hours, I sweat it out and start to worry that my people aren't gonna show up in Screven County. Maybe I'm wrong about this whole new party-hosting possibility. Finally, at the appointed hour, I drive up with Devon, my homie from work at Georgia Power, and we see the parking lot is *full!* Hell, yeah! We circle the parking lot and check out the line. There are girls and guys waiting. Next think I know, I get to watch the Exotic Girls greeting patrons, creating a buzz of anticipation. So far, so good!

By the time I made my entrance, the Exotic Girls at my side, the DJ had everyone chanting, "Kountry Wayne!! Kountry Wayne!!" The music was pumping through all the speakers, the drinks were flowing, and after I got on the microphone, and played my CD single of my theme song, "Kountry Wayne Swag Right and Everything," there wasn't a square inch on the dance floor. It was beyond anything I could have imagined.

Everyone started asking, "When's the next party?"

B-wood didn't exactly congratulate me, even though he did great business that night. I figured he'd get over whatever issue he had. But that was not to be the case.

As for me and the Exotic Girls, they gave us $300, saying it was a "test run." From then on, I made sure I got a large percentage of the door wherever I went. For the next three years, hosting parties became my Legit and Fast Money. It wasn't enough money to get out of the streets completely. Not yet. But for an idea that had sprung to life from my imagination, inspired by the women I knew and loved, it couldn't have gone better.

And the next parties would take all of us up to the next level.

How'd I know it would play out like this? Instinct. Knowing. There are all kinds of ideas that come to us all the time. They're like little daydreams that gallop across our brains. Sometimes you might get an idea that's so over-the-top, you know to ignore it. Other times it's just a vibe that sizzles in your spirit and tells you—jump up on it and ride!

More and more, I was learning which ideas were which.

Not only was I absolutely on the right path, but I was bringing others on it along with me. In less than a year, the Exotic Girls were being followed from club to club. We started with five members and eventually got up to ten charming, lovely young women who went from the Kountry and the projects practically overnight to being celebrities in southeast Georgia and parts beyond. Every female of drinking age with the stamina to *parteeee* wanted in. The Exotic Girls became influencers before that was even a thing.

By late 2010, I had moved in with Gena at her place in Statesboro and had encouraged her to have her daughter, Taylor, move in with us. Before long, I asked to help raise Taylor. Gena resisted at first. But my point was that if I was gonna be in her life, I couldn't imagine not being in her child's life, too. I knew what it was like not to have a daddy around and to watch my momma struggle. Even if Taylor wasn't my biological daughter, I wanted her to know that she was gonna be raised as one of my own. Smart, strong, and vivacious, like her momma, Taylor has been a blessing in my life ever since.

Gena turned out to be a bangin' mom—making sure that Taylor had the structure and support she needed to be happy and successful. Once Taylor was with her on a day-to-day basis, Gena began to see her own possibilities differently. She refused to depend on me as her sole support, but now she didn't have to worry as much and was freed up to do something she wanted to try—and become one of the Exotic Girls. In early 2011, I hosted my first party in Statesboro and it was Gena, already popular around the City, who brought the locals.

It all came together around my twenty-third birthday when I was getting my hair cut at Gary's Barbershop in Statesboro. As I was sitting in the chair, I looked up and watched as everyone in the shop spotted a guy walking in and, one by one, greeted him: "Hey, Hollywood! What's up?" one person asked. "Heard you opened up a club," someone else said.

Hollywood nodded and replied, "It's called 'Platinum Lounge.' Open for business."

Hollywood—real name Hayward Fields—was very much the Man in the City. An older cat who had been in the military and had done well in the construction business, he had that paper for real. You could call him Kountry rich.

One of the barbers asked him, "Do you know Kountry Wayne?" and introduced us.

Hollywood grinned. "That your Crown Victoria in the parking lot?" As soon as I told him it was, he brought up the fact that he knew I hosted parties and asked if I'd be interested in hosting a party at Platinum Lounge for the New Year.

I shrugged and asked if I could have a look at his club. A day or so later, I went to see it and was impressed. It was upscale. Like a real City club. But I'd also done my homework and had found out that nobody in Statesboro was showing up at Platinum Lounge. Another club, the Pond, was getting all the love.

I wasn't sure how we'd do on a Friday night in January—when it was cold and everybody was partied out from New Year's—but I really liked Hollywood. So I said, "Let's do it," and started to spread the word. The Exotic Girls got on their phones and called all their friends and the response was fairly positive.

In the short time I'd gotten to know Hollywood, I'd learned that he was real and could teach me a lot. He trusted me to help put his club on the map and I didn't want to let him down. In the time to come, he gave generously to me as a mentor and partner. He always reminded me of an older, more sophisticated Ice Cube, as if the rapper/TV star retired to Statesboro after having a rich, adventurous life. Hollywood had other businesses, including a construction company and real estate holdings. There was so much I was excited to learn from him. More than anything, I recognized a key leadership trait in Hayward Fields— the ability to follow through and bring whatever he undertook to completion. He was an example of how to work legit that I'd never been able to study up close. He had a wife and kids, a comfortable lifestyle, and an eye for enlisting other people's talents.

Hollywood saw something in me that he felt was worth his mentorship. He seemed to really like my hustle. All he said was, "You move differently from people your age."

There are two easy ways to find a mentor. First, pay attention to people around you who have wisdom in what they do or how they live. Ask them your questions. Better yet, follow them around and listen with your eyes and your ears as they do what they do. Second, if you see someone who might be younger or who is eager to learn, be a mentor to them. In the process, you will be learning to mentor yourself.

One night as I was talking to Gena about how to get people excited to come, she suggested, "You could promote the party on Facebook."

This was a new concept for me. "Like, for free?"

Gena said people did it all the time. You could post a notice about an event and invite people who would say yes or no or interested. Other people would see that their friends were going and say yes. The idea was golden. Before long I started to see the numbers going up by the day.

And more help was on the way. Between the Exotic Girls and me, we filled Platinum Lounge with three hundred customers just from our contacts. Then, at the last minute, the club got another wave of one hundred fifty more people.

What?!

Torrie found out that the Feds had busted the other club in town for selling liquor without a license. I'm not saying it was B-wood who snitched about the Pond but I did hear that B-wood told Hollywood there was gonna be a bust. His line to Hollywood was, "You good. They say your license is legit."

And that wasn't the end of B-wood's troublemaking.

It worked out to our benefit that night because most of the customers from the Pond made their way over to the party at Platinum Lounge. Everybody acted as if it had suddenly appeared in their backyard like magic and they'd never heard of it until that moment.

For the next four months, I felt like I had hit the club party–hosting jackpot. Every weekend from January to April 2011, I was throwing parties at Hollywood's club, getting on the mic, playing music, and watching every girl in the Exotic group get to shine.

My familiar callout, "It's your boy, Kountry Wayne, swag right and everything," was enough to get everyone to rap along. I was starting to offer a voice of encouragement, telling people to taste their dreams and go get it.

But then came a twist when I learned about why you have to "be careful what you wish for." The reason was that I was getting too hot in the city. Pops warned me, "You put too much spotlight on us." He was right. I started to chill a little bit.

When I told Torrie, she agreed it was the right thing. In fact, the timing was right, she said, because some of the Exotic Girls had decided they wanted to run their own business.

Say what? I could have been hurt. I could have put up a fuss. But then, I wouldn't have really learned what it means to give money and love unconditionally. Putting the Exotic Girls into orbit was something that wasn't done every day in this world. I gave an opportunity to a group of women with the intention that they might be able to shine in a way they never had before. It was given without strings or conditions—and that freed me to enjoy their success as much as mine.

Torrie told me that being part of the Exotic group had let her and the others see themselves as stars and feel great about themselves—earning money, having fun, seeing everybody in the club have a good time. They didn't have to use their bodies to get money or feel desirable. They could love themselves and give to themselves unconditionally.

Twenty-three years old, I had been given a gift that money couldn't buy—the chance to bless the women I love, and to see my sisters feel differently about themselves, something no man had ever done for my momma.

Give Unconditionally

To put this lesson into action, my advice is to start by thinking about the ways that you got to give unconditionally in the past. If you are having love problems, you do not have to respond by withholding love and money. When you have an expectation that you are going to get the same love back that you have to give, that's not giving unconditionally. Now, if you've been giving everything to someone who doesn't appreciate your gifts, cut that undeserving fool off from your good love and give it to yourself unconditionally.

Buddy loves women, no doubt about it. Yet he gives with strings attached. Drip actually pulled a Buddy move one day when he saw a beautiful woman filling up her gas tank and offered to fill up her car—only to be shocked at how expensive and how much gas her BMW took. Drip's simple feeling is, "Yuh, I treat people how I want God to treat me, for real."

In your business dealings, I'm not advising that you give everything and expect nothing in return. What you can do in the world of business, though, is look for ways to create opportunities for someone who needs a door opened or who might benefit from your guidance. If someone gives you practical wisdom, don't hoard it. Pass it on. Help someone you don't even know.

Practice the art of giving without conditions. Some people will thank you and others won't, but that's not why you do it. When you see that person reach further than they even knew they could reach, then you know you have shared the best of yourself with them.

All of that said, it is not your job to be in savior mode. That was one of the hardest truths I ever had to face.

CHAPTER 11

THE PLAYA LIFE

Life May Not Be Fair, But God Always Is

In Hollywood, California, one of the first things you hear about who gets famous and who doesn't is this line: "Nobody knows anything." Apparently, there is no surefire secret for success in show business. You might be gifted, handsome or beautiful, charismatic, hardworking, and even have the right connections—but somehow you are never at the right place at the right time. Or maybe you get a big part, but the movie is a flop. The same uncertainties happen for rappers or dancers or comedians, or in other fields outside of Hollywood—stockbrokers, car salespeople, clothing designers, entrepreneurs, you name it.

There is often no rhyme or reason as to who gets to win the big pot of gold at the end of the day and who doesn't.

The same can be said for how some people grow up with privilege and others start in the mud without much hope or help. When the cards get dealt, sometimes you get a great hand. Sometimes you're given more heartache than any one person should ever have.

None of it feels fair. You know what? Life is hardly ever fair. But that's why we all can take to heart that *life may not be fair, but God always is.*

The first time I went to Hollywood, as an up-and-comer, I couldn't even get arrested. I didn't fit in. *Nuthin* was fair. The movie industry said, "No Mr. Kountry Wayne or anything else Kountry." But God had a different plan and assured me: *You gonna be richer and more famous than all them LA stars.*

Up until the year I turned twenty-five, for the most part, I'd been able to feel God's love and fairness every day. But occasionally I had my questions. Why did my momma have to die? How was that fair? Why did the mothers of the brothers I love (my daddy's other baby mamas) resent me so much and wish me ill? Why did there have to be racism, violence, poverty, and inequality? The answers led me back, time and again, to the fact that humans are flawed and life is just unfair. But what do you do about it?

Fixing the problems of the world is not supposed to be all on you. If you do your part, you can make a difference. I believe that. But the problems of unfairness that most burden us are the personal ones.

If you wanna live the playa life—whatever that means to you—why waste energy being mad that you don't get *everything* you want and then complain that it's unfair? Why blame your situation on somebody who is competing with you? Remember: Don't hate the player, hate the game. More than anything, why give up on God? You may have been dealt bad cards, but you've also been given the know-how to make the most of what little you do have.

Life wasn't fair at all when my daughter Christiana was a baby. I'd only been with her mother one night and for a while I didn't know that we'd conceived a child. When I did learn about her later, I heard that, at birth, the doctors said she wouldn't be able to live past five and she would never walk or talk. Her mama called me when she was three years old and said she was walking. But I was crushed to learn that at age six the authorities had placed her in an orphanage because her mother wasn't equipped to take care of her.

At night, I'd wake up in a cold sweat, haunted by the guilt of not being there for one of my own children. This was when I was becoming famous and I didn't even want to make it in Hollywood because it wouldn't be fair to live that life if my child was living in an orphanage. Over the next two years, I had to fight the system and go through all kinds of legal red tape, going to court and everything, to be able to adopt her and care for her. The obstacles put in front of me were unfair and not in my child's best interests. But God, in His fairness, gave me the will not to give up. And so at the age of nine, Christiana was finally able to come and live with me.

The doctors had her on so much medication, I was convinced that had delayed her development even more. But when I questioned the meds she was on, the doctors only suggested putting her on more.

"No," I said, "let's try something else." And against the opinions of authorities and everyone I knew, I proceeded to get her off all medications. Overnight she began to improve dramatically and soon emerged as the miracle child she is. Other than needing hearing aids, Christiana was as healthy as you or me. She was eventually even able to attend regular classes at school and keep up. She's able to run, play, laugh, and communicate just fine. She is a flirt, too. I don't know where she gets it from.

Life was unfair with Christiana's deal of the cards, but God was there for her—guiding me to be the daddy I needed to be, willing to fight to have her close by so I could care for her. At first, having Christiana under our roof was difficult for Gena, especially as I started to travel more and more. My cousin Jackie knew my career was getting busier and wanted to help. With her own unconditional love to give my daughter, she begged me to let Christiana stay with her when I was on the road—an answered prayer. The double blessing was that Jackie's grown daughter later came to live with me and helped me look after the younger kids when they were visiting or when I needed an assistant on the road.

My point again, God—your Higher Power, the Universe, or whatever you call the One who resides in your spirit—is always fair. God is so fair we can't even wrap our brains around how fair and forgiving He is, and how loving and how much he wants good for every single one of us.

That is true whether you have lived the life of a sinner or a saint. You may not have a history of being a hustler or living the unapologetic Playa Life, but each one of us has our own share of sin and saintliness. The beautiful thing is that if we choose to sin a little less, or a lot less, we are free to seek the wisdom and the guidance to do so. How fair is that?

When you do choose to change yourself, you will dramatically change and improve your circumstances. I'm living proof.

Triple Threat

For three years—from 2011 to 2014—I was a triple threat. First and foremost, I was a rapper—really starting to get that mic to blow up, thanks to figuring out how to promote songs and videos on the Internet. Plus, my real-life fan base was being built live and in person through my role as a party promoter/host at Platinum Lounge in Statesboro, Georgia, which fed into my online popularity. Music wasn't paying off just yet and the party hosting still didn't bring in enough money for me to quit hustling.

Honestly, I wasn't out there dripping with paper to throw around or buy luxury goods for myself. My monthly overhead ate up most of the income—with my top priorities still about taking care of my kids, their moms, and whoever else needed it in my family.

Whatever else I could hold onto, I spent on myself—mainly on music and video production. I learned to find good people and pay them well. My reputation as a playa had been earned honestly, meaning I had to look sharp but not too City slick. So I used my money carefully. And the thought about luck running out on hustling days was never far from my head.

One familiar question nagged at me: *How am I gonna come up with another legit income stream?* That's all it would take for me to stop hustling. Whenever I tried to brainstorm, *nuthin* came back. I was stumped.

As the Lord is my witness, I never wanted to stay in drugs forever. It's just what I really knew about, and it gave me the fast means to afford the life I wanted for me and mine, along with the means to get where I wanted to go. There had to be a better way. Whenever I'd get down about it, I'd hear my daddy's voice telling me we were just gonna hustle until the mic blew up. Until then, I'd have to continue to use the illegal money to finally buy me a legal life.

By 2011, my visits with Judy Rocker were getting *awkward*. We talked a lot about the unfairness of sentencing at different points for my daddy, my uncles, and, before long, three of my brothers. She agreed that Black defendants were given fewer chances and longer jail sentences, more and more. We disagreed about how unfair it was that private companies were building for-profit prisons—creating a demand for convicts to make money and getting the government to foot the bill. Nobody I knew ever got rehabilitated while locked up. If anything, the time behind bars hardened the people who got sent away for nonviolent crimes. Judy's job was to prevent that from happening. She believed incarceration didn't have to be a revolving door because, she said, people can change.

Then Judy would use me as an example of getting out of the wrong world, of finding a way to support all my kids and pursue my dream, now that I was hosting parties and promoting Kountry Wayne in the clubs. She was proud of how it was all starting to come together. Whenever she said that, I'd nod and say, "Thank you." But deep down I wasn't proud of lying to her.

When Judy broke the news that I was going to be reassigned to another probation officer, I was sad not to be seeing her on a regular basis. But, *phew*, I was relieved not to have to lie to her.

My new probation officer didn't need to see me often because I managed to keep my name out of the streets even if I was still in them. When I did meet with him, I asked, "Is there any way to have my probation shortened? Time off for good behavior?"

He laughed. He didn't think so, but said he'd check into it.

Here's the deal: If I did happen to get caught while still on probation, I'd be headed for a mandatory eighteen-month sentence in lockup. Straight to prison. No passing Go and collecting my money, no Get Out of Jail Free card. If I wasn't on probation anymore and I got caught for anything, I would get a trial and be treated more like a first-time offender.

When I left the courthouse that day in 2011, I thought hard about what else I could do to be able to afford to quit hustling. My imagination started coming up with some funny ideas, none of them doable. But as I was driving back to Statesboro that day, I heard myself say out loud, "I could be a model." *Why not?*

At this time, Atlanta was an even bigger, more bustling City than it had been when I was growing up. Showbiz was poppin' and I had heard about acting and modeling agencies that were sprouting up. Atlanta was becoming the Hollywood of the South. The hip-hop scene was producing big names, TV shows were being shot, and, because of tax incentives, entertainment industry people were fleeing California and New York and heading to good ole Georgia. I did some asking around and next thing I knew, I was invited to a group interview at Atlanta's John Casablancas Modeling and Acting Agency.

Pops so happened to be doing some business in the area and decided to come with me. In a way, he was more excited about me expanding from music into modeling and acting than I was.

The two of us got there early and were told to go ahead and wait in a conference room. We watched the room fill up with mostly sophisticated-looking young people who held their headshots or carried portfolios. For a flash, I considered leaving but before I could, the woman in charge arrived and began to sell us on why we'd want to be with the agency. She encouraged all of us there that day to sign up for the classes they offered, whether or not we got signed by them as clients. The classes cost a lot! Then she started to talk about what they were looking for in their star clients. Looks were important, of course, but more than that, the key ingredient was having the drive to make it to the top.

Drive? That was me! I looked at Pops confidently. How could anyone resist my face or my confidence?

She then had us go around the room and asked us what it was we needed most to make it in Hollywood. One by one the other applicants talked about staying consistent, studying their craft, and learning how to audition.

When it got to my turn, I wanted to say that all I needed to make it was God. That was in my heart and on the tip of my tongue. But trying to be politically correct and safe, I said, "Hard work." The agency people looked impressed. But I immediately felt bad because I'd missed an opportunity to live my truth.

When we got back out to my car, I said to Pops, "I don't know why but I stopped myself from saying it's God who is all I need to make it in Hollywood."

"Son, I feel the same way. I had my hand raised and I was gonna say God is all you need but I put my hand down."

We didn't say much more about it, but my regret weighed on me. Why did I hesitate from giving praise in public? Well, I didn't have the answer. They later followed up with me, but something told me my path as an entertainer was going to go a different way—yet to be revealed. And that was that.

Over the next couple of months, I realized that my connection to God, as Momma had once told me, didn't require me to go to church but was all mostly self-taught or what my grandmommas and the preachers said about God, Jesus, and the Bible. I did appreciate the fact that preachers were entertainers—the way that they used words, rhythms, and gestures to guide their flocks.

A little light bulb went off. Maybe instead of getting the second-hand version, I should go to the source myself. Like always, I was given a sign. That same week, I noticed my niece had left her Bible at our place and that very day, I picked it up, sat down, and began reading the first page. I'd never heard about the difference between the Old and New Testament so I didn't differentiate. The first book was Genesis. I loved the word itself and the first line that followed: "In the beginning, God created the heaven and the earth . . ."

I was hooked. Addicted. Within a year, I had read the Bible cover to cover, both testaments. Not in one sitting, of course. Every day I'd read a lesson and try to see how that story could be applied to any number of problems in my life and in other people's lives. I saw myself in Jesus and in his disciples, in David and in Moses. I related to Job and to Noah and definitely to King Solomon, who was as rich as he was wise.

When I first started to read the real chapters and verses of the Bible, I was almost mad. I went and talked to everyone who had ever told me what was written in the Bible and I corrected them. Take the story of Samson. Getting it secondhand, I thought that his strength came from his hair. *No!* His strength came from his faith. Delilah cut off his hair to make him think he'd lose his strength and then he questioned his faith. The story of Samson was exactly what I needed to know to have faith that God would be fair.

I loved the story in the Gospel of Matthew when Jesus was trying to sleep during a storm and his disciples were sure they would all drown. Jesus didn't like being woken up, but he spoke into the storm and said, "Peace be still," and calmed the waters. That's what I learned to say to myself and know that the storms of life were getting ready to be calmed for me and mine.

One of the most profound passages I read was in Deuteronomy. It told the story of the hunger and thirst brought on by wandering the desert without food or water—when God told Moses to relax and the Israelites were sent manna, which fell down from the sky:

So He humbled you, allowed you to hunger, and fed you with manna, which you did not know nor did your fathers know, that He might make you know that man shall not live by bread alone; but man lives by every word that proceeds from the mouth of the Lord.

The teaching that we do not live by bread alone made me sit up in my chair. This was the beginning—aka the genesis—of me caring in ways I hadn't before about what I put in my body. These stories were better than any content on TV or at the movies or elsewhere. After that first year of reading the Bible cover to cover, I called my daddy and said, "I made it."

It was like I climbed the tallest mountain in the world and had returned with all the secrets of success. The very next day, I started reading the whole Bible all over again, right back from "In the Beginning." I read a lesson every day, right before I wrote in my blessing book, and as I continue to do so to this day. At this writing I am finishing up my eighth time through.

Each time, I get a new understanding and a new truth about how to live better and how to be a better parent. I like the teachings that your body is your temple and your health is your wealth. Most of those passages were practical, more than anything. Solomon gave the advice that you should quench your thirst, by all means, but not overdo it—as in, all things in moderation. My interpretation of Solomon is that he believed it was permissible to indulge in pleasures but not to excess. Why would he say that? He believed in a balanced life, meaning you can't be too holy in this world because you'll be no earthly good. You can't be too wicked because you will forget who gave you life. Solomon led the example of staying somewhere in the middle: Drink a little wine, quench your thirst, enjoy, have fun. Live life. Don't overdo it. I did try having liquor on my twenty-fifth birthday. *Mannnnnn,* I got drunk. Not for me! I like to have control.

Being moderate when it comes to coochie, now, that's another story. Then again, once I stopped eating meat, my lustful animal appetite seemed to downsize. That's a good thing because I was taking "be fruitful and multiply" a little too far. Now I know a lot of y'all might wonder how a Kountry boy like me later became a vegan—it was mainly 'cause, as a teenager, I hit my lifetime max of eating cows, pigs, chickens, rabbits, squirrels, and anything else that has beady eyes, hooves, or claws for feet.

By the way, the Bible is not all heavy and deep. The language is a little old-timey, but there's action, adventure, sex, and lots of drippy passages. Plus you will improve your vocabulary.

That first-time reading the full Bible was like a cleansing. Or so I said to my daddy afterward. My soul felt unburdened and thirsty, literally, for good, clean, pure water. You could just imagine wandering in the desert and then drinking from a spring bubbling up from a natural well that God has shown you in the wilderness. I became a vegan over the next three years or so, as my taste for meat slowly left me. I had already stopped eating pork in 2011 and was done with beef by around 2013 or 2014. No dairy after that. The last to go was chicken in 2015. Somehow, I didn't feel right eating God's creatures or having to kill an animal so I could eat. Someone asked me later on, "Oh, so you are vegan, huh?"

"Uh, is that what they call it? I thought I was a vegetarian."

The person was nice enough to tell me the difference. Since I was eating a 100 percent plant-based diet, that meant I was vegan. I was proud to live the Vegan Playa Life.

The other interpretation of not living by bread alone is that we should not live by money alone. The first time I read that passage, I was reminded, in his fairness, that God will send us what we need to move us along to the next place in our journey.

What had I been sent to give me leverage? Opportunity. The money I earned illegitimately got me a seat at the table. But the ace up my sleeve—what let me be the Man in the City—was the God-given sauce. It was the drip.

The funny thing I learned during this time is that the entertainment industry doesn't care if you have some money or no money. They want the sauce. They want the drip. That's what led to me starting to get agents and managers who believed my rap career would open other doors. That's what led me to Chase Walker, aka DJ Southanbred, or just "Bread" as I call him. He directed the video for "Playa Life," a single from 2013. He and I have worked together ever since. On a limited budget, he captured the sauce of the song and the story to perfection.

Southeast Georgia went crazy for "Playa Life." We didn't wait long before we followed up with a single release and a video of "Twerk Alert." By 2014, my dad's prediction that the mic was gonna blow up finally happened. This fun song was a club record all the way, capturing the wildness and twerking of the club dance floor. Thanks to the local following, plus fans sharing my content on Facebook, and paid promotions to Atlanta radio DJs, I made it to the big time.

Hearing my voice, my lines, my rhymes, on Atlanta radio the first time was, as they say, like I died and went to heaven. I remember celebrating at a party I was hosting one night and becoming all emotional. I had a hit single on the radio. It was almost too much to believe.

I was on top of the world. My real version of Playa Life was coming true. I didn't think it could get any better. And, in fact, it didn't exactly.

Much to my surprise, fair or not, things just got a lot more complicated.

Fifty-Fifty

The problem of how I was gonna get out of the streets had a new solution: One night in the summer of 2014, the club owner and my friend Hollywood gave me a call and raised the possibility of us going in together to own a club. Platinum Lounge had been shut down months earlier and he had a new vision.

He had become a mentor to me. And I helped him stay current. He avoided drama and knew how to stay up. We were well-matched partners.

"Let's go!" I was all the way in.

The idea was that if I paid for the labor, initial rent, and other costs—approximately $10,000—he would contribute construction materials, know-how, and almost $35,000 worth of liquor. We'd split earnings fifty-fifty. This was a huge gift, but a sign of how much of a scene I had created.

A for-real club owner. Me? At that moment, I could not have thought of anything more legit and more secure. I had the people and the streets. Hollywood had the experience. My first call was to Gena. She loved the idea. Then I got Queet on the phone and she was so proud. My daddy and my sisters came next.

After feeling almost delirious for hours, I realized that any plans to retire from hustling were going to have to be put on hold *again* so I could afford to open up a club. But this was just a delay in the short run. Once the club opened, I'd be making Successful Business Owner money!

Hollywood had picked out the perfect location. It was where I had thrown my first party—the Legion. B-wood had gone out of business in Screven County when I started throwing parties at Platinum Lounge and then had tried his hand opening a club in Statesboro, called Primetime. When we announced that we were opening a club where the Legion used to be and calling it Tha Spot—"If you at Tha Spot, ya hot, and if you ain't, ya not," B-wood got shook.

With my money on the line in the legit world, I, once again, pulled back from being too much out and about in town in any kind of flashy lifestyle. The truth of it is that reading the Bible had toned me down somewhat already. At least some. Gena and I had our ups and downs through this. But we were still together, and our place had gotten a lot fuller with the arrival of our new daughter. Melissa, named for Momma, is as pretty as can be, and may be the funniest of all my kids—who are all funny. Her imitation of Drip, later on, hit it out the park.

One of the larger complications had occurred earlier, in March 2014, when Pops, who was watching my back, making sure I wasn't getting too much attention, forgot to watch his own.

Apparently, whether or not anyone snitched, the police were following him that night. And while he's on his way to make a drop, he gets pulled over with drugs in his car. The police are about to handcuff him and take him in to print and book him, when my dad Vincent "Skip" Colley, not in bad running shape in his early forties, bolts and starts to hightail it out of there. But he's not fast enough. They catch him, cuff him, and beat him so bad they can't take him to a jail cell. He's messed up. They have to drive him to the hospital in Millen. His girlfriend Cheryl gets there, then calls me and I arrive very concerned.

His eyes are bloodshot red, his face is all swollen, and his watch is falling off his wrist, but he is surprisingly coherent. I say, "Pops, they beat you, huh?"

"Yeah, they beat me."

The police are trying to explain why they had to get rough because he ran and they had to wrestle him.

Lucky thing Pops had an eightball with him earlier, before the police nabbed him, and he had dipped into it enough that he was feeling no pain. As soon as the police leave the room for a minute, my daddy tells me in a hushed voice where the money is so I can go get it.

Before I hear any more, the doctor comes in, with officers close behind, and says Pops needs to be moved to Augusta because his injuries are so severe. Now the police are starting to look bad and decide to rush my dad out of there.

The story I hear later is that as soon as he is in the hospital in Augusta all hooked up to monitors and IVs and bandages, the doctor in charge of his care refuses to let the police go in until the next morning. So they wait. Only before they get to go in the room this time, the doctor asks to see the arrest warrant. The problem is they don't have it— because in their haste to apprehend him they forgot to fingerprint him.

It's already the middle of the next day and, to make matters worse for the police, they not only have to leave to go get a fully executed arrest warrant, but they're grumbling over the fact they won't be able to get it until the following morning. Meanwhile, Pops calls me over at Jackie's house where I'm staying.

He tells me what's happened. In between pauses because he's having trouble breathing, he says that prison will kill him. "I can't go back in," my daddy says. He knows he's facing at least three years.

Because it's my job to save the day, or so I think, I tell him, "I'm gonna figure this out." Then I get guidance from above. I even went home to read the Bible. Heavy. Then I call him back at nighttime, knowing the police are coming for him.

"You need to leave," I say. There's no arrest warrant, nothing that would say to the hospital that he's running from the law. So he does what I tell him to do, pulls out the IVs and the tubes and manages to sneak out of the hospital with his girlfriend. A couple of hours later, at Jackie's house, there's a knock at my door. It's Pops and his girl-friend.

That moment was an awakening. My days of being the guy to save the day had to come to an end. The time had arrived for me to remember that, though I may follow Jesus Christ, Pops could be saved only through His grace and love. Whatever the plan was gonna be, I had to surrender to God's fairness.

People like to say, "Let go, let God," but we have trouble with the letting go. We want to backseat-drive with God at the wheel. I started to practice saying, "Let God do it," because even if I tried to control the outcome in certain situations, there were so many pieces of the puzzle that I knew *nuthin* about. God's not in the *trying* business. He is in the *I am* and *I will* business.

I turned over my father's concerns to the Lord in faith.

Pops knew he had only bought some time and he would have to turn himself in eventually. But he knew how to lie low. Besides, he really wanted to help me build the club.

To this day, I wonder if someone tipped off the police. I'm not sure who that would have been. But I do know that once Tha Spot opened, B-wood would be aiming to get my club shut down *fo* certain.

That meant we all had to be even more careful. Good thing that God had an even better plan.

Power of Prayer

We have all heard the saying that if you give someone a fish, he'll eat for a day, but if you teach him to fish, he'll eat for a lifetime. I guess that tells you it's always better to be a fisherman than a fish. The lesson ignores the fact that if a man doesn't eat fish at all, that could be unhelpful either way. But the point about fairness is for you to understand that the mantra of "Help Is on the Way" doesn't mean you are going to wake up and find a refrigerator full of fish if you are hungry.

If you are doing everything in your power to provide for yourself and your baby Drip-lets—as Drip would say—then your Higher Power will arrive on angel wings to give you help. Prayer is also more powerful when it's specific. My prayer for a long time was Kountry simple. I wanted a legit income stream. When I wanted to really change my life, my prayer was that I wanted to know God more.

According to many spiritual belief systems, the one thing you can't pray for is for something that's already happened to be undone. Because that would be assuming that God made a mistake, which is impossible.

Life is unfair and cruel. But God is fair, loving, and accepting. All the time.

I have friends who ask me to pray with them because they don't have the words and I am humbled when they ask. I only have one true prayer: Let God's will be done in your life.

Buddy fails at prayer and that's how it is with him, but Drip understands that God is fair. He might make a joke, pointing out, for instance, if you broke your ankle, "Yuh, be thankful to God you can't walk outside and be hit by a car in two days."

Using humor in prayer is not disrespectful. Who more than God could use a good laugh now and then?

CHAPTER 12

DIVINE COMEDY

Don't Get Mad, Get Money

This next principle requires me to admit that, in the past, I have found ways ever since I was a child to turn the haters and non-believers in my life into my enemies. I made a list. Then I proved them wrong, checked them off the list, forgave them, and, whenever possible, made them my friends and allies. This approach served me well when I moved to Hollywood and made the system there my enemy, left, and then came back with the secret to fame and fortune of *don't get mad, get money*.

All that time being mad gave me an outlet for my frustration and, I confess, also gave me some good comedy material. But, at the risk of telling you something you already know, when you let somebody or something make you mad, you give them power over you. It's wasted energy, even if it drives you to grind harder than you normally might.

But just consider how much better you would be using your energy if instead you chose not to get mad, but to get money.

In other words, get to it! Whatever gets you that paper or that exposure to opportunity or that income stream that feeds you, go get it.

Don't get mad, get money is another way of saying "Success is the best revenge." I like to say that comedy is the best revenge because you can get rich from turning your enemies, or the parts of yourself that aren't flattering, into funny characters.

In the beginning, the character of Drip was never too far from me in actual life, but, as time went on, he and I have taken seriously different paths. It's been rewarding to see the massive reaction to those Drip videos. The character has gotten so popular that at one point I was even able to drop a real-life Drip rap album in collaboration with famed Atlanta producer Zaytoven. It's a crazy world. Drip and Buddy started to dominate the storytelling so much, in fact, that in time I would have to pull back from them so I could keep growing and be the face of my own comedy. But, *mannnnnn,* I'm not complaining about the revenue Drip's been generating!

The moral of the story is that when you decide not to get mad but to get money, you may have to switch up how you do the getting. For instance, you do not have to chase that money, you can let that money chase you.

This is a hard concept but sometimes there is such a thing as trying too hard to go after money. Sometimes, when you chase it, that money's gonna run. Everybody nowadays is working on their brand, pitching ideas, monetizing their content, selling merch. You don't wanna chase so obviously. Let money chase you. Be excited about your brand, your merch, your content, of course. But be cool. Be exclusive. It's like chasing a woman. Instead of throwing yourself in her path everywhere she goes, let her show up trying to see you. If you put the work into yourself, she'll come. She'll notice.

Chasing a man or a woman will usually result in you getting him or her. But you'll be his or her last resort if you did the chasing. Don't chase the game, whatever it is.

One of the best ways to apply the lesson of not getting mad but getting money is to see the humor that you were ever mad in the first place. Really, if I had not learned this lesson, I would never have gotten out of Millen. If I had not learned to see the humor in all the things we say and do when we are mad, I wouldn't have had a lot of material for a comedy career.

You're probably waiting to hear the story of how that came to pass. And, well, because you are my favorite audience, here we go.

Turning Up Viral Edition

Having the inspiration for the Exotic Girls and then the ideas for becoming a party promoter and eventually a club owner were major flash points that helped turn everything up in my life and career. And the next breakthrough idea was even bigger—so much so that I found myself realizing I was about to go viral! September 2014 was when *all* the pieces come together.

Let me back up. *A lot* was going on. For starters, Hollywood, aka Hayward Field, and I were working around the clock to open up Tha Spot in Screven County. Keeping a low profile, Pops helped out, too, whenever he could. I was grateful that God had given my daddy a chance to be a part of this process. Sooner or later, he was going to have to turn himself in, but to be able to be part of helping build a legit business for his son. That was a gift.

At this time, I'd been getting hot under the collar because B-wood had opened up a club—in Millen, of all places—and asked me to throw a party there. Hell, no! I got mad and chose not to get the money.

"Y'all come to my city and open a club without even talking to me? And now you want me to throw a party for you? I'm the Man in *this* Town and I got the people in *these* streets and they'll be coming to *my* club . . ." That is the PG version of what I really said.

Hollywood and Pops got me to calm down. We didn't want any bad energy to get in the way of our smash-hit opening in December. Real fast, I switched to don't-get-mad-get-money mode. Luckily, I had a distraction that was leading me to my destiny. Wouldn't you know? It happened because of a girl.

I can hear you: "*Really, Wayne? A girl!*"

She was a young woman, beautiful, and she was not interested in me one bit. But my momentary crush on her changed the direction of my life in ways I could never have predicted. We'd first met in Atlanta, where I'd gone to promote "Twerk Alert," which was still on the radio. At that point, I was getting hot in the City of Atlanta—getting booked on TV for rapping and receiving lots of female attention. But this lovely ladeeee, named Kayla, was apparently unimpressed.

I can remember my confusion, as I ran into her and some friends and stood there thinking, *I don't get it. I've got my sauce and my drip. I'm fresh, got a pocket full of money, at least a couple thousand on me, and Kayla and her girls are talking to me, but kind of shining me on.* Suddenly they saw this dude walk by and started buzzing like I wasn't even there.

"Oh, y'all know who that is, don't you?"

"He looks familiar. Who is he?

"He's a comedian. DC Young Fly."

"He's cute."

"And hilarious."

My inner monologue shouted at me, *Mannnnnn, I'm the playa from the Himalayas, standing here with this money and y'all looking at comedians?* It was like I'd missed that news flash. Girls were getting hot for the comedians now. How did they even know he was funny?

Kayla showed her phone to the others, who began to coo like turtle-doves. One of them pointed to the YouTube fan count, saying, "He got a lot of fans!"

It was like the clouds covering my eyes lifted. It all clicked in my mind. Comedy was more important now than having rolls of money and cars or jewelry or even hits on the radio. The old game was over. You had to get fans in numbers that could be counted to be truly legit.

Damn, I thought, *I could do comedy.* I knew I was funny. All my family members were natural comedians. Whether they knew it or not.

Besides, I was the biggest comedy fan and student in the world, starting all the way back in Head Start. Momma must have planted the seeds for this calling for me when she made sure we had cable, no matter what. She nurtured that interest by letting me consume nonstop hours of comedy while wearing out our VCR. I could claim to have watched *all* of Eddie Murphy, *all* of Martin Lawrence, and *all* of Jerry Seinfeld. Even though my comedic experience was from the Kountry, Seinfeld was relatable to me through his subject matter—mostly about relationships but also about people's ridiculous pickiness and pettiness. Seinfeld basically played himself, or an exaggerated version of himself, and used his real-life story as a stand-up comic to frame every episode of his sitcom. That in itself was an education in how observational humor in stand-up comedy worked. Just as influential was everything I learned from watching sketch comedy like *In Living Color* and *The Jamie Foxx Show.* Come to think of it, the Exotic Girls were kind of inspired by the Fly Girls, who warmed up the audience before the sketches got going on *In Living Color.*

The more I thought about it, the more I realized comedy had been my superpower all along. My freestylin was known for its flava of being fun and funny. Hosting parties in the club was partly a warm-up for my comedy career. I'd go so far as to say that my comedy instincts had saved my life and kept me out of dangerous situations ever since early childhood. My slogan ought to have been "Don't get mad, get funny." Now it was time to get funny and get money, too.

It was still a mystery how to do that. How did any newcomer break into the comedy game without years and years of hanging out in comedy clubs? How did first-time comics build an audience and earn a rep to be taken seriously? Well, I knew how to get fans in the rap game but that cost money to make money.

The reality right then was I had no money to float myself to explore a new career. In fact, by Labor Day 2014, I'd spent everything left over after expenses to promote "Twerk Alert" and gambled away $3,500 I'd just earned hosting a club party. It must have been my old habit of wanting to get that Fast Money.

I wasn't panic-stricken because I knew the club would be earning a profit in no time. But I also knew this was a crossroads for me and I needed to get quiet. As in the past, I decided to take a few weeks off and to go spend time with my children. I stayed away from the streets as much as possible and let Hollywood keep the work going at the club to get ready for the December opening. During that downtime, I found out how anyone could make a "vine"—a short and funny skit. With your phone, you could shoot a video and upload it onto Vine, a social media platform, or you could upload your video onto Facebook or YouTube.

After watching lots of user-created content—some good, some so-so, some worthless—I decided that this was something I could do. Why not? My kids made me laugh so hard, about everything and anything, and I started to get some ideas from them for videos of my own. The feeling was like I was being guided. It was almost eerie. What else under the sun could I do, other than comedy, that would allow me to pull real situations from my own life?

My first Vine came from hearing stories of how guys would call home to their girlfriends from jail, and my technology for shooting it was back from the Stone Age—a regular handheld phone camera. I just did a comedy monologue, acting like I was making the call from prison and talking about how, once I got home, "You can go through my cell phone, I'ma stay home every night, and I'm thinking about marrying you." The character I was playing was an early edition of Drip—without the swagger.

My first viewers were my homies from southeast Georgia and some of my new fans from Atlanta. I couldn't tell how many people exactly had seen the video, but the comments were encouraging. A couple of days later, I shot a Vine of a guy being pulled over by the police and saying all kinds of crazy stuff out of being nervous. Again, it was just me, straight to camera, being silly. The funniest part of the video was that my daddy, a for-real fugitive from the law, was the voice of the cop. The comments were even more encouraging. I guess people could relate.

From there it was off to the races. I had funny ideas for videos flowing from my brain all day long. Since I was working, for free, as the sole actor, they were cheap to make, too. My comedy concepts covered child support, baby mamas, late bills, bill collectors, the birds and the bees, dating, sibling rivalries, and whatever else I felt like talking about. I had big plans—even though I had no guarantee this was going to turn into anything more than fun.

During those first couple of weeks, I noticed that most of the more-popular people on Vine and YouTube posted a video every day or every few days. Without knowing it, I had stumbled onto a hint of an algorithm. The best way to explain this term is that it's a mathematical formula for how things flow. If your content was relatable and accessed by a group of people, who then shared the video, your views would keep multiplying—as long as you kept the flow going with new content. What Mark Zuckerberg and his team and other social media gurus understood very well is that it's possible to go viral with one video, but if you don't sustain it with an additional, steady flow of content, you'll be like a one-hit wonder. The good news was that in Millen, where I'd been the Man in the Town since high school, I had a built-in fan base that was watching me. So within a week, I started to get a handful of likes from my posts on Facebook, but it wasn't until two weeks went by that Facebook added a new feature that allowed you to see how many views your video had gotten. Up until this change, I had never thought about how many times a video had been viewed. This was huge.

One day I went to the bathroom with my phone—because I was checking it constantly—and saw this new feature and was impressed that the video I'd just posted had two thousand views. That was more than half the population of Millen.

It was like some kind of magic. Facebook would then ask the user who had viewed the video if they wanted to be a follower. All that meant was that my videos would be in those people's feeds every time I posted. There it was—the answer to how I was gonna get followers. All this, just in time for me to start putting up videos? No way was it a coincidence! In the middle of the night, I picked up the phone and called Prince Tay, waking him up out of sleep, almost yelling with excitement. "Tay, this is God!"

"What is?"

"They done started putting views on Facebook. I'm gonna take off! God's opening up Facebook for me!" I went right to citing the Bible and called it the parting of the Red Sea for my exodus from an old life to a new one as a comedian. "I told you the Bible real!"

Now, in addition to skits, I was posting real life comedy videos every chance I got. Back at work at Tha Spot, I'd take a break and shoot a little something, showing the wall we'd taken down and how we were building a bar. "Hey, y'all this is Tha Spot, Screven County, about to be the hottest club anywhere in southeast Georgia!" I'd pan the room and show all the workers and say something funny about them. My engagement with local viewers held steady, with a few thousand views per video, until October 11, 2014, when the viewing pattern did something *very* different on my latest funny skit. The idea had come to me from a real situation. Now that I was cutting out meat and butter from my diet, the women in my life weren't sure how to cook and had made some dishes that tasted like cardboard.

So I put that into skit form. What if a girl cooks a meal for her boyfriend and it's terrible, but he has to pretend it's good? It was Kountry simple. The camera was on me, just looking out to the audience and asking for help with my eyes while trying to eat this plate of plain, unappealing baked potato. In the skit, the girlfriend is in the background asking, "You like it?" And I'm faking it, "Mmmmm, yeah . . ." while she's gonna get me more—so eat up!

The video started out by getting the usual two to three thousand views. That's what it said when I checked it one Saturday morning before I took a shower. When I came back, there were ten thousand views. Hmmmm, hold up. I had errands to run that day but when I came back it was at thirty thousand views. Was it a fluke? That night I was hosting a college party at Georgia Southern University and getting a good reaction. Everyone started coming up to ask, "Yo, Kountry Wayne, when's your club gonna open up?" That meant they were starting to engage with my content, my life, in addition to being club goers.

"First weekend in December," I promised—but then glanced back at my phone. Up to fifty thousand. *Mannnnnn,* I thought, *I'm about to be famous and they don't even know there's a celebrity in the house.*

Here's a clue: When the views are local, you cap out—because everybody knows everybody and you are engaging with the same folks. Eventually, you have to get outside of your local community if you want to grow your audience. But something out of science fiction happened that night. The algorithm kicked in and jumped to other users who liked or viewed similar content but in faraway places. Comedy is global. Funny is universal. Didn't matter where viewers came from because everyone could relate to the situation. We all have some Kountry in our blood. All of a sudden, views for my newest video were coming in from New York City and Miami and Salt Lake City. There were views in Canada, Israel, Japan, and countries I'd never heard of.

That night the video hit two hundred thousand views. I had gone viral.

From that day forward, I put up two or three videos a day, and continued to do so for two years solid. That was the same day I ended my rap career. The truth is I was good. My dream of being at the top of the rap game had sustained me through times when to some people I was just a Kountry dope dealer who was never gonna be legit. Rap helped me create a platform, but it was not the destination, only the vehicle. Without any regrets whatsoever, I jumped off the rap boat and landed on both feet on the good ship of comedy. The crazy part was that being funny had always been in my blood, but it had taken a girl to reject me first for me to see that being funny was actually my calling.

Word to the wise: Don't let a rejection make you mad. Instead, get the money. Maybe that rejection is gonna show you to yourself in a brand-new way.

Don't get mad, get money was starting to make sense—even though the money, as far as I knew, was bringing me fame and not actual paper.

I'll never forget working at Tha Spot that week and trying to fix some ceiling tiles. Feeling so happy about the video going viral and about becoming a comedian, I used a phrase that had been in my head for years: "Help is on the way." I wasn't being funny, just real. "Hey, this is my club, Tha Spot. We'll be open first weekend in December and it's gonna be the hottest in the city! Look, I want you to know, no matter what struggle is goin' on in yo life, keep the faith, 'cause help is on the way!"

That phrase has been the theme of my life, fo sho, but I'd never said those words out loud. Suddenly, they became my anthem. I even started singing "Help is on the way, help is on the way," from the Whitney Houston song. From that point on, whenever I was hosting a party, people in the club would ask me to sing it and then they would sing it along with me. RIP, Whitney.

It kept on going. Besides the escalating numbers of views, I was gaining seventy thousand followers a week. When Hollywood and I opened our club the first weekend in December, we combined it with a twenty-seventh birthday bash for me. We made $8,000 our first weekend and $10,000 the next weekend. We paid ourselves back that first month. Unheard of! The happiest person of all was my daddy. He was beside himself.

That night I was up to 250,000 fans. It was miraculous. The gates to the future had opened and I had people believing in me.

Nuthin like this had ever unfolded in my imagination before. It wasn't just me having a legit life as a businessman. This was getting rid of the family curse, clearing the way for my kids and everyone else in the family.

In March 2015, I hit one million followers.

I didn't know how crazy and fast all of this had been. I didn't know how it was gonna support me, either. All I knew was, a month later, I started getting requests to show up at events and big parties or clubs just to make a personal appearance. I didn't have to host or MC, just to walk through as me, Kountry Wayne, and create buzz. One club owner down in Cuthbert, Georgia, even smaller than Millen, offered me $1,500 to come down to the sticks and mingle for a minute. For me, the money wasn't the point. This was my first chance to see if I had really gotten famous off the Internet.

I saw Pops on my way out of town. "Be cool," I warned him. He'd been good about flying under the radar. So much so, I didn't know where he stayed most of the time. But every now and then, I knew he'd forgotten he was a fugitive from the law and we had to rein him in.

When my brother Crenshaw and I got to the club in Cuthbert, I was in such a hurry to get inside and see the impact of going viral that the owner had to remind me, "Kountry Wayne, hold up, lemme pay you."

How they crammed that many people in there, I don't know. I do know they felt like they knew me and my life. That was the impact of the viral videos. They quoted a few lines from the videos and made me feel like I was in my own hometown, like they'd met a star who'd really made it big, but was from the Kountry just like them.

It was finally dawning on me how getting famous online has the potential to be profitable in the real world. Over the next couple of years, it would be even more evident.

Life in the Spotlight

The more successful I became in the legit world, especially as a club owner, the more I realized how easily things that go wrong can put you out of business. In fact, a shooting outside the Platinum Lounge had forced Hollywood to close his doors there. Later, when I had two clubs jumping at the same time, we had a shooting death outside one of the clubs one night that didn't shut us down but was tragic and should never have happened. I had avoided guns and violence all my life and this really upset me. Whenever anything like that happened, I'd go sit in city council meetings and try to save the business while reassuring the good citizens that it would never happen again.

Then I'd have to go to these meetings and hear complaints about the noise. None of the people complaining would come out and say that they were mad because these were Black-owned businesses. I'd just hear these old Kountry white ladies sitting next to their husbands, talking about, "Bubba and I cain't sleep a wink!" Both clubs were out in the boondocks. One of them was near a truck stop and nowhere near as loud as the freeway noise. But I wasn't getting mad. My job was to listen, show concern, but keep on getting money at my business.

When Hollywood and I first opened our place together, the plan was for him to let me run it and for him to kick back. But suddenly, I got so busy because I done got famous that Hollywood ended up running the club. We didn't hear much from B-wood or his partner, even though I could imagine he wasn't too happy when he couldn't get any people to come to the new place he'd opened in Millen—because they were all over in Screven County at Tha Spot. It took a lot for me not to rub it in, though. I didn't want the negative attention. I felt like LeBron James when he and the other members of the Miami Heat finally beat the Boston Celtics in the Eastern Conference. Hey, competition is good for the game, whatever it is.

In March 2015, to my great relief, my probation officer informed me that my request to be done with probation would be granted. All I had to do was pay off the $800 bond and they'd record me as having completed the ten years in seven years. Done!

That was a huge load off my mind. But I also knew that if I didn't get out of hustling, once and for all, I would be madder at myself than I ever had been at anyone else. Though I was tapering off, I hadn't yet figured out how to get out of the dope game for good.

At one point I went to this one store where I usually bought supplies for packaging the product and was startled when somebody pointed me out there, saying, "Kountry Wayne, swag right and everything!"

My stomach dropped. Now that I'd gone viral, I realized it was really only a matter of time before the police—who were my fans!—would get word that I was still dealing. My legit business as a club owner was bringing in as much as $20,000 a month, giving me $10,000 as my share. That was also the same amount I needed to make every month to meet my bills and family responsibilities. I just needed one more regular cash infusion every month to replace what I'd lose if I did go fully legit. The bigger issue was that if I quit hustling, Pops would have no income and I couldn't be his sole support.

And that's how I came to get a second club. When the idea first hit, I asked myself, *Could I do that?* Nobody had told me that I could or could not be in comedy, so why couldn't I open up my own club? The minute I put on my entrepreneur hat, I heard of a location in Oak Park, Georgia, and decided to go for it. This was not Fast Money, meaning it could take me months to get it going. And even if I was the sole owner, I couldn't do it alone. Whatever was gonna happen to Daddy, I wanted him to have a piece of it, 25 percent. My brothers and sisters could work there, and my baby mamas, too, if they wanted. Family business. The location was far enough away that it wouldn't compete with Tha Spot. That's why I decided to call it Tha Spot Two.

I also started to receive messages from other club owners and booking people at comedy clubs asking for my fee. My what? They were talking about my fee for doing stand-up. They were throwing out terms like: Can you do a half-hour set? Can you do forty-five minutes? Wait a minute. Up to this point, I only made three-minute videos. I had no act. I didn't even tell jokes, really. Opportunity was being offered but I couldn't take advantage of it. For one thing, I had no time to respond to the requests. For another, I didn't know what to ask for.

Well, help was on the way. A bit earlier, not long after I hit one million followers, I got a call from a woman in Atlanta by the name of Ona Brown. She was a motivational speaker, a success coach, and she hosted a radio show in Atlanta. Ona wanted to invite me onto her show so she could interview me about my insights as a rapper-turned-comedian and business owner.

When I got there, I found it was AM and nobody much was tuning in. But it did give me an opportunity to right a wrong.

While we were on the air, one of the first questions Ona asked was, "What's been the one thing you used to make it?"

I flashed back to two years earlier when I wanted to say God but had chosen not to speak my truth. By a strange stroke of coincidence, this studio was housed in the very same building where the modeling agency meeting took place. What do you know? I'd been mad at myself ever since. Here was a chance to stop being mad and get on this moment. The first word out of my mouth on the radio was, "God." Ona encouraged me, and I must have said God, Jesus, the Bible, in every other sentence. God, God, God, Jesus, Jesus, the Bible. Timing is everything.

And I haven't stopped. If you've seen any of my stuff, you've probably also seen all my #God and #Jesuspoppin tags, too. I could have kept going with #Mosespoppin, #Allahpoppin, #Buddhapoppin but instead I settled on #love.

Ona told me over lunch that she was a personal manager for actors and models, and she said she might be able to help me now that I was getting hot online. She was not saying, "I want to represent you," just that she could respond to some of the requests I was getting.

Normally, she would have picked up the tab for that lunch. But when the waiter dropped the check off, I pulled out a roll of bills—about $3,000—and took care of it.

Ona barely blinked an eye, but I think she was surprised. As I paid the check, I said to her, "Well, we gonna do this?" Apparently, there's a whole song and dance for doing Hollywood business. But I needed someone like her. Right away. Ona, the beautiful daughter of motivational speaker Les Brown, agreed and, in return for 20 percent of whatever I made, said she'd call the places and get me some bookings.

Other stand-ups later expressed some resentment. They'd worked their way up the ladder after starting at the bottom rung, doing open mics, perfecting their five minutes, and having to audition just to perform for free. They'd knocked on doors and been rejected by agents and managers until finally they'd achieved their lucky break. In six months, I'd gotten further than many of them.

To be honest, I could have been mad if I was them, too. But I really didn't know any different.

My first gig was on Mother's Day of 2015 at a banquet hall in Fort Myers, Florida. Ona had negotiated a fee of $5,000, less her commission. I was probably too ignorant to be nervous, but I went there with my pride and charisma, expecting to be spontaneous and just be myself.

I was a little concerned that no one would show. But the person who hired me had promoted my appearance and as soon as I arrived, I saw that the venue was over capacity. That was a good sign. Being myself, I went out and started to tell stories about my kids, Millen, not being able to pay bills, and women problems. The laughter was scattered. I imitated some of my uncles and that got me a few more laughs. After a while, I said, "If y'all don't laugh, I'ma strip down and get buck naked." The laughter started to swell. "You think I'm kidding?" With that, I began to take off my clothes for real—and everybody howled. Uncontrollably. Maybe it was the delivery, but I had them. Then I went back to telling my Kountry stories without my shirt on.

Barely missing a beat—with Ona's help—I started to book live gigs every other week. I definitely did my homework and started to write jokes and come up with an act. None of this was a huge jump from hosting parties. I knew how to hype up a crowd, using music, dancing, physical bits, and even funny sound effects. My business instincts kicked in as I got to know my audience. In particular, as far as language, I decided to work clean. As far as subject matter, I was relentless. Somehow when you tell a drippy joke with a Kountry accent it sounds pleasant. And funny.

By the end of the year, just as we were getting ready for the opening of Tha Spot Two in Oak Park, I was making a profit of thirty to forty grand a month easily, between comedy shows, hosting parties, club ownership, and hustling. This was all enough for me to finally get out of the streets.

My birthday bash 2015 was a glorious celebration. *Really,* I thought that night, *if this is as far as I'm gonna go, this is the mountaintop.* My eight children, at the time, were healthy, happy, and loved. I was on good terms with all my baby mamas and I was actually starting to talk about setting a date to marry Gena.

Everybody was there. Everybody who drank got drunk. Everybody who didn't acted like they were drunk anyway. We danced all night and didn't care if Bubba and his missus couldn't sleep.

That night I told Pops, "I'm gonna go legit real soon." He was happy for me but it was bittersweet because I was leaving him in the wilderness by himself. He wound up staying there and living in the club with one of his girlfriends for the next couple weeks.

He might have pushed it longer, but in a couple of videos that I'd been posting, apparently my daddy had somehow gotten into the crowd scenes and someone in the family noticed it. The Feds were gonna knock on our door any minute.

In January 2016, I had a Friday night gig down in Brunswick, Georgia, and the day before, Pops called me and asked, "Son, okay if Nicole and I come to the show?"

It was a big risk. My dad was gonna drive his 1987 black Grand National that was just a billboard on wheels advertising his whereabouts. I tried to convince him to get another car or even not to come. All he could say was, before he got caught and went to prison, he just had to see me do my thing on that stage one last time. The mic had blown up, just like he had always said it would. He wanted to come so bad, I couldn't tell him no.

"Yeah, c'mon down to Brunswick, Pops," I told him. "Be careful."

Right after we hung up, I got a twinge. Something told me that I shouldn't wait until February to clean house. Wasting little time, I got my brother Tay to wipe the place clean and to give away anything of value to someone who needed it, just to get rid of any trace of drugs or any paraphernalia. Prince Tay got it done.

The very next morning, *sho 'nuf,* there was a loud knock at the door. One of my family members answered it. Standing there, with a search warrant, were FBI agents asking for me. I came to the door and they asked if I had any idea where Pops was staying and I said, "I don't know *nuthin.*" They searched the place from top to bottom. They found *nuthin.*

Pops had been on the run for two years, but obviously the writing was on the wall. The Feds had everyone close to him watched. One of the FBI agents left a card with his name and phone number to give to Pops when he turned up.

Before I left to drive down to Brunswick that afternoon, I called my dad, told him what had happened, and gave him the phone number, and urged him, again, to lie low. Instead, Pops called the agent and said he would turn himself in on Monday. He told them, "I just wanna see my son do his show one last time before I get locked up."

The club that Friday night was packed and the show was smokin' hot. Right at the end I looked over at Pops and announced, "Shout out to my dad who's in the house tonight. He's turning himself into the Feds on Monday and doing the right thing so I'ma hold it down out here while he's serving his time." The crowd gave him a roaring applause.

After the show, I hugged my daddy hard. He laughed so much, he said, that he forgot all his problems and he felt kinda free. We started to walk out to our cars and Pops all of a sudden put his hand on my shoulder and said, "You've been a much better son to me than I was a father to you. Thank you." He said he was so proud of me.

I told Pops that I was proud of him for doing the right thing. And then I, Mr. Fully Legit Entrepreneur and Comedian, swag right and everything, got in my car to drive on to the next city and the next show, and then rolled down my window and called out.

"See ya on the other side," I hollered at my daddy. "Three years ain't *nuthin.*"

Hometown Celebrity

As an example of how powerful it is not to get mad, but to get money, I want to give you one more piece to this part of my story. You will know how to apply this lesson to your life far better than I can tell you.

This is a lesson that Drip, my once-upon-a-time alter ego, can't learn. When his rap career takes off, he gets offered a good sum for just showing up in the club, but he wants to get paid in full up front. The club wants to pay him half up front and half later. He doesn't know how to get past being mad and just get the money. Buddy, on the other hand, hardly ever gets too mad because he got the money and he writes the rules of his own game.

Being mad can give you a fire that's undeniable, but it will burn you out in time.

After becoming officially legit, I didn't really know how much I had changed until a couple of months later when I was at a restaurant in Millen, grabbing a bite before leaving town to do a big comedy show.

Who did I see over at a nearby table but none other than Brad Adams. He was with some other police officers. One of them came over and congratulated me on my success, with my nightclubs and everything, and said he enjoyed "Twerk Alert" but he couldn't get enough of my Facebook videos.

"Thank you," I said, and shook his hand. Over at the table Brad just scowled.

My food arrived but I had to get up and go over to Brad to interrupt his meal. When I tapped him on the shoulder he stopped, looked up, but didn't say anything.

"I just wanted to thank you, Brad. If it wasn't for you, I wouldn't have become as successful as I am today." He looked like he was about to say something but didn't. So I added, "I'm 'bout to go headline a comedy show and I'm gonna make more money than I ever did selling drugs!"

Brad smiled—or made an effort to smile. From then on, in my mind, he was no longer an enemy. He's an important part of my story and I say his name whenever I count my blessings.

PART III

CHAPTER 13

THE LAST COMEDY SHOW IN THE WORLD

What Don't Kill You, Just Don't Kill You

One of the perks of growing up in poverty, in the mud, is the lesson I want to share with you now and it's probably already in your wheelhouse. No matter how far you've traveled from your humble roots, it's good to remember when things go wrong or seem heavy that *what don't kill you, just don't kill you.*

When I first visited Hollywood, I could barely follow the California accent. The women especially have a way of shaping words with their whole face—like they're imitating an emoji. I was fascinated. In a California accent, you can say something that people have been saying for years and it sounds fresh. A lot of people would say, "What doesn't kill you makes you stronger." That sounded hopeful. But was it true? Naw, not in my experience.

The fact is you can go through many things that come close to killing you but don't. Just because you got beat down does not mean you got stronger. Plain and simple, what don't kill you, just don't kill you.

Lemme put it this way: As a parent, no matter how chill and faithful we are, worrying about our kids can age us overnight. But loving them and being protective is not fatal.

There's another way I use this lesson and it's when people give me a hard time for having so many kids and baby mamas. Look, we all have sins of our own that shouldn't bother other people, so I say if my sins aren't killing you, they aren't killing you. Me having children and taking care of them doesn't harm you. I also am a believer in a woman's right to choose whether she wants to bring a child into the world or not. Women are put through so much day to day, I say give them the respect they deserve to make their own decisions—and stand by them and be supportive however you can. Now, with all that said, I am fully aware that the drugs I was selling did cause harm and heartache in many families, including my own. The truth is that my choices could have killed others and my rationalization—that I did it to get out of the mud—was wrong. In fact, it was only when I stopped hustling for good that I was freed.

If your choices bother you, look to make a way for someone else not to continue the cycle. Or you can use this lesson to cut yourself some slack, if, let's say, you didn't handle everything in your relationships as well as you might have. You may have just been doing the best you could. You can look back and see certain things differently but take comfort in knowing that what didn't kill you, didn't kill you.

We can learn to apply this rule when it comes to our own shortcomings or when things really go haywire and all you can think to do is run and duck for cover. I learned this lesson early in my life but I had to relearn it in a whole new way.

Stay Grounded

The four years between January 2016 and March 2020 were jam-packed. My comedy career blasted off like a rocket ship—straight into the stratosphere. Almost immediately I went from performing in smaller or lesser-known venues to top-name comedy clubs. Before long I started crisscrossing the map of North America. Just as my video storytelling had struck a chord with folks from all backgrounds, the same connection happened out on the road. Comedy, again, crosses all barriers. Wherever I went—from Honolulu to New York City, from Edmonton in Canada to Houston to Detroit and DC—I brought the Kountry with me and turned those cities into Millen. Before I left, I'd become the Man in the City there.

There was a lot of temptation. It was still a surprise how crazy women will go for comedians. Rappers, action-adventure celebrities, superstar athletes—all those dudes I get. But there's something about seducing females with humor . . . apparently it's like irresistible foreplay. Comics got it goin' on!

I did enjoy having a fling or two with some very talented comediennes. But it's not sexy time when y'all get competitive over who's funnier in the bed. I toned that down real fast. Given my track record, you know I was never good at saying no to women. But I really did decide at one point to work on my lust problem. The first year of committing to that goal I flunked out fast. Well, what don't kill you . . .

The women in my life who put up with me and love me anyway are saints, especially the mothers of my children. Most of them know me and accept me for who I am. But that doesn't mean they take it in stride. Neither do I. In 2017, I felt that I was ready to be reformed. Somewhat. Or at least I decided to save myself from myself, and, after long last, marry Gena. We were expecting another baby—a daughter—who was a ray of sunshine and magic from day one. I named her Honest because she was my first child to be born when I was living honestly, not hustling. By that logic, I ought to have named my other kids Cheater, Liar, Womanizer, and so on, but I couldn't do that to them, really. Honest was the first child out of nine up to that point who would grow up without her daddy's background in the streets as part of her story.

Seven years earlier, I'd promised Judy Rocker I would hire her to plan Gena's dream wedding, and I kept my promise. We went all out with a fairy-tale setting, like something from a movie. But my bank account had a change of heart, so we decided to go to a justice of the peace instead. The wedding money went to buying Gena a Benz, which was her dream car.

At this stage of the game, I was no longer a club owner. For one thing, I didn't need the money from the clubs and it wasn't worth the headaches. For another, I knew that for the clubs to be run the right way, I needed to be in Statesboro on a more consistent basis. More and more, I was on my way to the next comedy club in the next city. Or I was heading to Hollywood for meetings and auditions. At this time, I switched to agents and managers on the West Coast, who urged me to get a place in LA.

"Y'all know I just got married and have nine kids I gotta see?" I asked. They understood and recommended I commute to see them on weekends. So I went ahead and got a place in Studio City at a gated complex with lots of show business types. Everybody was on their way to being somebody but wasn't much interested in anybody else.

I got a little homesick for nosy, small-minded people back in Millen.

Commuting between Georgia and California was not great for my marriage. But if anyone knew how to grind, it was me. And when I had a chance to do my first tour in 2017, I said, "Hell, yeah!" It was for 150 dates, which kept me on my toes. It was a comedy master class, as I learned on the fly to try out new jokes or embellish bits I was already doing. I called it the Child Support Tour because it literally just paid my child support. The travel and coordination became so complicated I hired my brothers Arby, Tay, and Crenshaw to come on the road with me. My act improved expeditiously from where I had started. My goal was to build every show up to the point where, by the end, everybody was partying in their seats and laughing to the point of tears. I'd have one of my brothers come out as a DJ at the end and put on a record that got everybody up on their feet. I'd pull out bits from my party-hosting days and every show was like a comedy revival.

When I went back home, I'd crash, hang out with my kids, and get caught up with other family members. When I could, I'd make more funny videos and post them. They didn't make me money per se, but I needed to continue to build my online following—because those followers were helping me sell tickets in live settings. Gena and I were great when I was back home. She's a wonderful mother, as is Queet, as are my other baby mamas. Gena and I didn't do as well when I was back on the road. That was on me.

By 2019, I faced the reality that our marriage wasn't working. Gena was too tough to show her heartbreak, but I felt terrible for letting her down. All I could do was take the responsibility and try to be a better human being. What don't kill you, don't kill you—but it *sho* can hurt.

No sooner had we gotten all the divorce papers finalized than we both had regrets. I knew this was probably not gonna work and that I should try celibacy or declare myself for the streets, but the chemistry between Gena and me could never be denied.

That's where we were in January 2020 when I headed off on my North American People's Champ Tour—which was going gangbusters—until everything suddenly came to a screaming halt.

Last Comedy Show in the World

Maybe you remember what you were doing and where you were when you first started hearing about coronavirus. COVID-19. Was it bad? Was it *nuthin*? Was it a flu? Maybe you remember nobody knowing anything except that it was coming like a tsunami wave and we were all on the brink of a shutdown due to the pandemic.

I was in Norfolk, Virginia, late on a Saturday night, getting ready to go on stage for what I thought could possibly be the Last Comedy Show in the World.

The day before, Friday the 13th, of all dates, when the national emergency was declared, I had flown into Norfolk. For the previous week or so, I'd been getting mixed messages about whether my gig at Chrysler Hall's Festival of Laughs was *on* or not. Months before I was so happy to accept a spot on a bill that was *hot*. I'd been climbing the comedy ladder from clubs to theaters and Chrysler Hall was poppin'. There were four of us: Sommore, a twenty-year stand-up veteran and "Undisputed Queen of Comedy"; another veteran, Tony Rock, host of *Def Comedy Jam* on HBO (and damn near every other TV comedy show); Gary Owen, who not only had a BET TV show but was dubbed by *Ebony* magazine as Black audiences' "Favorite White Comedian"; and me. Tickets for our one show, scheduled in the 2,500-seat theater, sold out so fast that the festival promoters added a second show.

Whenever I checked the Chrysler Hall online schedule, a new cancellation or postponement for March, April, and even May events had just been posted. Somehow, though, thank God, the March 14 date, come hell or high water, or COVID-19, was going forward. So it seemed.

Then, I got word that Sommore canceled. Before everyone else canceled, too, Lavell Crawford, of *Last Comic Standing* fame, replaced Sommore on the bill, and I breathed a sigh of relief. But only a small sigh. Next thing I knew, cancellations for my other March gigs started to trickle in.

Mannnnnn, I felt like this was about to be biblical. Something about the seven years of famine story came to mind. I'd been doin' great earning legit money on the road as a performer—over $1 million a year before taxes. But my monthly overhead was at an all-time high of $75,000 and every time I tried to put money away for a possible downturn in the economy, a new expense jumped up. The signs that night were telling me that the money from live performances was about to run dry for a spell. A short spell, we hoped. This wasn't just about me and my family, but if these live venues closed down for even a month, a lot of comics and other performers—athletes, musicians, and all the folks who work in those venues—were gonna be in a world of hurt. The big names aside, most working-class famous people have very little cash saved up and can't get by for very long without having a gig.

Damn, I thought, standing backstage at Chrysler Hall, waiting to go on for the Last Comedy Show in the World, *Am I fixin' to be broke?!*

Onstage, Gary Owen was making coronavirus jokes, all while wiping down the set and disinfecting his props. Earlier, the first show had been a little surreal. The laughter was there, *fo sho,* but it had an edge to it. Not everyone who bought tickets came out. This second show had even more empty seats.

Ever since Judy Rocker had given me a blessing book, I'd spent time every day being grateful for life and grateful for the opportunity to bless someone else. If this was gonna be the Last Comedy Show in the World, the least I could do was to give thirty minutes of drug-free laughter and escape to all these people who were about to go through their own hard times.

It was an out-of-body experience. The whole time I was onstage, I was flashing through my life and recalling all the lessons that had brought me to that day. When I took my last bow, to a standing ovation, I'd never felt so humbled in my life.

That night I received one of the most-welcome compliments from comedian Tommy Davidson, who for some reason was at the Last Comedy Show in the World in Norfolk. I'd been watching Tommy do his thing on TV and in the movies ever since *In Living Color*. He's definitely a comedy legend.

The fact that he took the time to say something was a big deal. A lot of established comics would call me an Internet comedian, and try to make me feel less legit. Hollywood had never really taken me seriously as an actor, either. Tommy gave me high praise. He said, "You're just so smooth out there, man." He said I was different and that this was only the start. During the show he had turned to my brother and said, "Look at him out there just killing it. Making it look easy." Tommy described me as a smooth criminal, and added, "A silent killer."

As good as Tommy's words made me feel, I had some pressing issues on my mind. All these talented comedians who were on the bill were walking around wide-eyed and bewildered. Were we like the last living survivors on Earth who skipped the pandemic by going to a comedy show? Or were we all gonna run outside and fall out from the virus there and then?

How bad was it gonna get? Who knew? Something in my senses told me it was gonna be brutal and that some people were gonna die.

In a way, that put the money problems in a kind of perspective. If it don't kill you, hopefully something else won't.

When we got back to the hotel, my brother Arby and I ran the numbers. Once I paid the monthly bills for March, I was gonna have $13,000 to my name. That was after shutting down my place in Hollywood, selling cars, and pulling back on boyfriends of baby mamas, who would just have to go apply for unemployment like everyone else.

"Got any other ideas?" he asked.

"Well, I guess I'm about to see if all that 'help is on the way' stuff I've been saying all these years is real."

He said, "Yeah, we 'bout to see if all the Jesus poppin' is real, too."

"Yeah, we shole is," I said.

Rock Bottom Is Not the Worst Place to Be

Sometimes it's not comforting to have to apply the lesson that what don't kill you, don't kill you. Lemme suggest maybe another way to think about those times when you hit rock bottom and feel like you've just performed at the last moneymaking show in the world.

It was in this place, by the way, that I soon breathed life into characters who were going to take on a comedy reality of their own in my new videos. They were born to remind everyone we'd been through hard times like this before. Buddy, an opportunist, made it work for him, as he'd point out: "Listen, I have a lot of flaws. Sometimes you might skip over me. Well, before you hit rock bottom, I got some rope made out of blue-and-white paper, with pictures of Benjamin Franklin on 'em and I'll throw you a line, little dahlin' . . . " Drip understands rock bottom and is ready for it with some bars: "I don't need no favor 'cause a favor could come from a hater who gonna talk about you later. I'd rather depend on my maker, yuh!"

Drip has the wisdom. He knows that you can be down-and-out or on top of the world but the best place to be is where you know *help is on the way.*

Rock bottom is not the worst place to be. Why do I say that? Because it's usually at rock bottom where you'll find God. For real.

CHAPTER 14

STRAIGHT OUT THE MUD TOUR

Understand the Difference between a Go-Getter and a Hustler

Back in 2018, I got to talking to Jordan Jackson, a comedian friend, and he said something that almost slipped right over my head. Jordan—who later opened for me on my 2022 Straight Out the Mud Tour—said, "Wayne, you should really be monetizing your content."

Up until that point I thought of videos as a way to build an audience for paid bookings. In my mind I was giving them a taste and getting them addicted so they would want to come and see my show in person. In fact, by 2018 and 2019, I was not pushing on the viral skits much at all because word of mouth about the live shows was filling seats and I was earning over $1 million a year as a stand-up. So when Jordan said that about monetizing videos, I didn't pay much attention because, honestly, I didn't want to put content out just to get a little extra money and possibly lessen the value of the content. Then I got to thinking he might be right.

I knew there was an algorithm—or the way social media moves in a flow—for going viral but I couldn't quite figure out how to understand the flow for making big bucks from ads placed in viral content.

So I did some testing with ads embedded on my Facebook content. Dang. A little while later I received a check for a small amount of money. It was like a taste. But I didn't really know what the next step was to make passive income from content. My problem was I wasn't thinking yet like a real hustler. I was thinking more like a go-getter.

What I had to review and relearn was *understanding the difference between a go-getter and a hustler.* (Hint: Albert Einstein was a hustler.)

I've been both a go-getter and a hustler at different points in my life. The Kountry simple explanation is that the hustler has a visionary mentality. The hustler has a vision for taking on an existing system. The go-getter works within that system, helping put the vision into action, or following the formula without really getting it.

In Hollywood, a go-getter will go and get the job, lots of jobs, and lose sleep working day and night. A hustler creates the jobs. A go-getter can be a valuable member of the team but doesn't run the show. Without a hustler, visionary, or entrepreneur, there is no show.

Joseph in the Bible was a hustler. God gave him the genius of prophecy and the ability to interpret dreams. When Joseph interpreted Pharaoh's dream to predict a seven-year drought and famine, he used his vision to create a system of saving up for the hard times ahead and then of rationing and conserving the grain. Joseph didn't just arrive on the scene to win Pharaoh's favor. He doled out his vision like a dope boy go-getter and a hustler combined. He built his reputation. He gave God the credit.

In school and in the streets, most of us are taught to be go-getters and to apply a rule or formula that everybody else follows. Few are taught to be hustlers, to develop visions of our own. In algebra, I could always get the correct answer, but I'd use my own system, one that the teachers could not understand. Most thought I just wasn't applying myself—sometimes they were right—but mostly I was ahead of my time.

So was Albert Einstein, who we can safely say was a genius, a visionary, and a hustler. As a kid, he was said to be creative and a problem solver. But he almost flunked out more than once and didn't get into a big-name college. So no one could have predicted that at age twenty-six he would come up with probably the most important scientific equation ever—$E = mc^2$—which led to the basics of the whole field of quantum physics and proved that a tiny particle of matter could create a massive quantity of energy.

Think about that. You might see yourself as a tiny speck in the universe, trying to make it somewhere as small as Millen, Georgia. But if you harness the hustler inside of you, just imagine the massive quantity of energy you can ignite.

That's why I chose this lesson as the last to cover because it's the one that got me from down at rock bottom all the way back up again to a record-breaking Straight Out the Mud Tour. It took my knowing when to go back to the basics of go-getting and when to take charge and rise up from the ashes, thanks to my own formula as a hustler.

A hustler or visionary—an entrepreneur who comes up with breakthrough ideas—needs go-getters to help build the vision into reality. Understanding the difference can empower you to know what the best use of your talents might be at any given time.

Spiritual Gangster

My version of being a hustler is as a spiritual gangster. First, at the start of the shutdown, I ran some thoughts by God and then took time to have heart-to-hearts with all my family members. I was gonna come up with answers, I told them, but everyone was gonna have to lower expenses and look out for each other. I got my teenage sons to come stay with me because I knew, with the quarantine, they'd go stir-crazy and be too much of a handful for Queet.

My parenting style is to love my kids but not to spoil them. If it comes down to my getting them a new car or getting one for myself, they are the priority. Always. But I'm stern. We have rules, chores, and responsibilities. They do not have to live up to the dreams I didn't achieve for myself. My prayer is that they become the best versions of themselves that they can be.

The first order of business was to apply for a Paycheck Protection Program (PPP) loan. It didn't take long for me to observe that a big need was going to be in the shipping and transportation of goods. See, that's the thing about being a hustler with ideas—you have to pay attention to the trends. I'd seen ads from Amazon that you could sign up to deliver boxes with your own Amazon truck. They were hiring like crazy and all you needed was capital to invest in your truck. The PPP loan was easy to get because it was the pandemic.

Had I ever owned a trucking company? No. But I'd opened up a club and run a few businesses. Paperwork ain't no thang. So we got the loan and had income within weeks. Pops, who had just gotten released from prison, became my top trucker. That was a good start, but it wasn't enough to feed all of us. Pops was the go-getter at first but eventually I let him take over and run the business for himself.

My vision, based on faith that I would be guided to my next moves, tested me, but I never gave in to doubt.

And finally, after about six weeks into the lockdown, I had an old-fashioned brainstorm one night. First of all, everyone was stuck at home, either unemployed or working from home, and here I was with a platform of about six million followers and I wasn't doing anything with it. Second of all, I flashed back to Jordan asking me why I didn't monetize my content. Why not take another, deeper look into that?

As a result, in May 2020, I took a real close look again at social media patterns—and in quantum physics time I changed the game. If ever there was a time when all kinds of folks needed to laugh, *this* was it. I did a little video skit of me calling my son's teacher and crying. I apologized to her for never appreciating how hard it is to be a teacher and "put up with these loud-mouth kids who just eat and fart all day." This was not really a hustle move. I was just using the system I'd developed before as a go-getter for myself. This was just a test. But the engagement was strong. That's when I understood that the Facebook algorithm was studying the users, their comments, their engagements, their interests, and their friends, then serving them the kinds of ads that would appeal, based on that data. So this told me something that blew the lid off.

To test it out, I did an interview with my daddy—real, straight from the heart, talking about our journey and how help is always on the way. It was longer than most of the videos I'd posted and was more spiritual than funny. Now that was me being a hustler. I was changing up my pattern and it bumped the algorithm. So now the ad robots are seeing engagement from other interest groups. But wait a minute. What was I doing in comedy and in being serious that made my content a good landing spot for an ad? Simple answer. Suspense!

I knew how to tell a story and have people wanna know how it ends. Oooooh, I gotta watch this ad so I can get back to my show. So that's when I knew that I had to think of my comedy skits as a series. I added more production quality, cast some incredibly talented actors, and became the Albert Einstein of my world. Drip had a cast of characters surrounding him. So did Buddy. And so did my character. The story lines were hilarious, yet taken straight from life.

In the middle of the shutdown, we tried to make you forget your worries. We ran a God-fearing set, stayed clean, played by the rules, and took it shoot by shoot. Remember, this was all new for me. The videos I had shot that launched my stand-up career were just me on camera basically. Now, I was thinking more like continuing story lines with characters played by me *and* others. At first, the idea was to test what worked and get other people's attention. In one skit, I played a cop and my partner was played by Chase Walker—who shot the videos. The viewers were there right away. So we added production value to up the entertainment. This was a throwback to when I was promoting the Exotic Girls and I knew the value of costumes, lighting, hair, and makeup, and I wanted professionals to do it right. We went so far as to buy a gimbal, or a mini steadicam, to hold the cell phone. We were rollin'.

Actually, my plan was to wait to get back to Hollywood and use the skits to produce a real TV show. Instead, because the pandemic shut us down for longer, I went back to putting out the videos online. My cast was mainly all my kids—who are all comedy geniuses—my brothers Arby and Tay, my sisters, and whoever else was around me. As a producer, I was grateful to have Kountry Wayne to work for me for free, and the flow of interest went crazy. Everyone wanted to be in the videos, not for money, but to get famous.

Chase gets a lot of credit for finding so much talent in Atlanta. He is a real innovative guy, and passionate about the film business. Chase had a smokin' career as DJ Southanbred for Solja Boy, but gave up being a DJ to make our videos. He was both a go-getter and a fellow hustler/visionary with me. When I told him about my idea for a cougar story line, Chase found Rolanda Wright, who brought her own character to life magically. Chase also found Blake Rogers, the love interest of my son Tony, whose story line evolved beautifully. When we needed someone to play the biological father she'd never met, Chase went out and found Mike (Michael Anthony), whose character has become a favorite to our fans. Mike is so funny he doesn't even know how funny he is—except, when he tries, it's not funny. We eventually were able to get T.I., Ludacris, and other celebrities to do cameos. Everyone who steps on our set checks their egos at the door and adds something special to the mix.

The themes we cover are universal—relationships and marriage, parenthood, jobs, business, competition, gossip, having a moral code, being a good citizen.

Creating opportunity for others is another difference between a hustler and a go-getter. God gave me opportunity and pointed out that everything I needed to get through this rough patch was already there for me. It wasn't a win for me if it wasn't a win for all of us.

At the beginning of the lockdown, I had 6.5 million followers. Two years later, when I came back from the Straight Out the Mud Tour, I had 11 million.

When you strike oil, I know sometimes it gushes for a while, then levels off. Well, that's what happened with hitting that motherlode during the dark days of 2020 and 2021. My first decent-sized monthly check from ad revenue alone was $35,000. The next one was about twice that. For a while that held steady. The next few months I earned $100,000, $150,000, and $200,000. By the following spring, I was at the peak and earned almost $500,000 in one month.

As we were coming out of the shutdowns, I went on an interview on *The Breakfast Club* in New York City and talked about Drip's new album and also about how I'd survived the pandemic. There was some skepticism in the room. Like, *Now what? You had $13,000 at the start and you made $7 million in how long? You bought a showplace mansion for all your kids?*

Then I had to explain how I'd gone from nine to ten kids. Yes, I was blessed with my eighth daughter, Kiyomi, who was born during the pandemic. The house is my grown-up version of all those dreams I had as a kid. Every one of my children has a room that was designed with his or her interests and tastes in mind. We have a swimming pool. But most Black people can't swim (some stereotypes are true) and every-body's gonna take swimming lessons. I'm also building a championship basketball court. My kids may be the only ones in the neighborhood who can't swim but they are gonna wipe the neighborhood with that basketball court.

A lot of people in the hip-hop entertainment world refused to be-lieve the $7 million was real. It threw me back to people in the City saying I was too Kountry to make it and the people in the Kountry saying I was too City.

What other people think of you is not your problem. Nobody be-lieved that Albert Einstein could have so many women throwing themselves at him. It was his hustle. His visionary system changed the existing system.

People will doubt you. The haters all thought I was pulling a gimmick. Like I had to be making it up or somebody was floating me all this money so I could promote my content online.

But I didn't care anymore. And I knew that once we all started getting out of our houses, the ad money would go down—and it did briefly. Once I changed the system, it was back up. I'll come off the road and get a message that my content has earned $600,000 for the month. Passive income! Get to it.

Just to show the genius of God, in early 2022, I was given a big opportunity to do a Live Nation Tour that took me onto some of the most celebrated stages of the country—the Apollo Theater in Harlem, the House of Blues in Las Vegas, and the Fox Theatre in my current hometown of Atlanta, Georgia, to name a few. Coming back to Atlanta for a sold-out show was a dream come true for a Kountry boy from Millen. It validated my decision to move to Atlanta, which is arguably the capital of Black entrepreneurship today. Not too many years ago, I would admire the successful professional people of color and their families that I saw on the street and only dream that could be my world one day for raising a family of my own. My kids and I have come a long way.

In go-getter fashion, I let the promoters do the promoting, but when the shows weren't selling out, I went online and used my knowledge of how to draw in the crowds. That's the difference between a go-getter and a hustler. We sold out everywhere and we even added a show in Vegas. The show got so much buzz everywhere. I found out later that I was the first of the new generation of Black comedians to sell out shows at large-capacity theaters with my name alone on the ticket.

So don't be shy if you see a way to improve a program. Let your hustle help.

Everywhere I went, I tried to really take in the audiences. A lot of people needed to come out and laugh. We are all coming out of the mud right now, if you ask me. We all can be each other's secret algorithm for success and help each other through.

Your Story Is Not Yet Written

In recalling all these turning points in my past, as hard as I worked to stay up, I would have drowned in a sea of misery at certain times—if not for the faith that help was on the way. My word to myself was that my story had not yet been written and I told myself that truth by building strength out of other people's stories.

So I just kept going day by day. I kept using that visionary formula that a small speck of energy can change the world for the better and that it's up to each of us to show how we want to do that. In believing that I could write my own story, I was able to get from point to point to where I am today. My most sincere hope is that you are given the same strength and wisdom to see that your story is not yet written—so it's up to you to get to it and write the greatest story your vision can deliver to you. Then be a go-getter and go get it.

Your story is the one that's going to inspire everyone who knows you—and maybe the next Kountry Wayne who doesn't want to be counted out. Whatever you want to create for yourself and the world, help is on the way for anyone with the courage to be a visionary. Whatever is in your mind to try, I say, "Get on down here and show us." Turn your ideas into businesses, into art, or entertainment. Whatever you've wanted to do—write your own book, be a motivational speaker, start a podcast, make a painting, show off your style, whether it's how you fix cars, do hair, or the way you manage your finances and achieve prosperity.

Sometimes I'll shoot a video of me dancing and I do it for me. So do your dance, smile your smile, and be a magnet to quantum joy. The Universe has got you. Don't forget to drink water and don't worry about what anybody else says about you. Keep my other top lessons close at hand—stay up and live your truth. Honor your mother and your father. Love one another. Love yourself.

WHY YOUR STORY MATTERS

One of the reasons I encourage you to embrace the lessons that have served you along the way and that will be there for you as you develop your vision for your one-of-a-kind dream-come-true story is because of your opportunity to positively influence the people in your love who matter most to you. Your story matters and why not follow lessons like Stay Up and Live Your Truth, and all the others, that show others how their stories matter, too.

Whenever possible, I try to encourage the people who are closest to me to ask themselves how they see their own stories unfolding, what kinds of lessons they've learned from my example, and what kind of example they hope to set for others. This subject came up as I was in the process of finishing this book and I was really inspired when I asked my kids and their moms and my family members what important lessons they've learned to date and how they hoped to see their stories come to life in the future.

The first responses came from my kids:

The biggest lesson you ever taught me was to not let haters get in my way of pursuing my dreams, not to doubt myself, and that everyone starts from the bottom. What I wanna do in the future, sports wise, is probably be in the WNBA (*never knows*) and besides sport-wise probably be a nurse, pediatrician, or a lawyer. —Alayah

The lesson you taught me is to believe and have faith in God, He is real. What I want to do with my life when I get older is to be just like you. —Zarhia

Biggest lessons—nothing comes easy and be consistent. My goals—actor and social media entrepreneur. —Temar

The biggest lesson that you taught me was to never give up on God and to be grateful because you never know what God got coming for you. Seeing the way you came from nothing to something was very inspirational for me because there's times when I feel like I'm not worth the time and energy. Seeing all that you do plus still making time for God, I know is not easy but you find a way, and I really love that about you. What I wanna be when I grow up is to be an entrepreneur and an actress. I wanna be across all platforms in the world and if that don't work out for me then God is gonna find a way for something even better. —Malia

Biggest lesson—to never give up and learn from every situation to be a better person. My goals include actor and influencer. —Tony

The lessons you taught me—not to be a follower, to be a leader and to be tough. I want to own a childcare center in the future. —Christiana

What you've taught me is to work hard for what I want. You've taught me this because you were not born into what you have, you've worked for it. My plan is to study science—Taylor.

The biggest lesson you taught me is to not be a follower and don't do what everyone else is doing. Dream—to be a professional dancer. —Melissa

Biggest lesson is to love God and eat vegan food. Dream—to be an actress. —Honest

Several of my adult family members and loved ones responded, too:

Lesson: Despite all odds against me, if I create a plan, write it down, and allow God to guide me, God will give me the provision to sustain it! Life goal: To become a multi-streamed entrepreneur, with a successful boutique. I want to be in a place so that my children, their children, and the generations to come, can ultimately benefit from me making a decision to bet on me and work hard at it! —Tilquisha

The biggest lesson Dewayne has taught me is to always put God first and to always have child-like faith. Having child-like faith leaves no room for doubt or uncertainty. You believe as a child would, disappointments are short-lived and quickly forgotten, and your hopes continue to remain high for great things to come. —Gena

Lesson: Have faith in Jesus. Goals: to have the best relationship possible with Him. —Arby

Number one thing I was taught by Kountry Wayne was to keep God first and stay up and win in everything you do, no matter what. Where I wanna be in the future is keeping God number one and being able to handle and control everything I dream and see myself having in my life. —Prince Tay

You've taught me the biggest steps toward "success" are God and our ability to believe in ourselves. You've always been confident and a risk taker. You bet on you! I want so much to be that way! Wholeheartedly! That's a rare thing to master for most of us!

My dream is to be a successful writer and business owner. I want to help others with the lessons I've learned. That dream never leaves. That's how I know it's God given. I have to do it but first I must believe I can. —Torrie

The biggest lesson you have taught me is doing nothing sometimes is something. To me that meant you telling me "Stop worrying you gone always be okay." My goal for the future is to own my own bar/lounge and that it makes more money than I could ever imagine and more than anything makes my family proud. —Shavonne

The most valuable lesson you ever taught was to totally rely on Jesus and don't rely on mankind & when you take care of your kids, God will take care of you. I learned what it means to really be a good father from you. I always wanted to live a stress-free life, not to have to worry about things financially. I never had *nuthin* particular that I wanted to be . . . I just wanted to live a stress-free life . . . but my wildest dream was to be a horse rancher. —Pops, Vincent Colley

I wanted to include these because it's my hope you, too, will have the experience of assuring the people in your life who matter most to you that their stories matter. Whether you teach them a lesson about faith or about pitfalls to avoid or how to stop limiting themselves or how to be able to stay up and live their truths, you will be reminding them that the best success is being an example to somebody else.

Give it a try. Wherever you are in your life, why not ask folks around you what you've taught them. Or better yet, ask yourself what they have taught you. That's a video series right there. Maybe even another book. The beauty of every day is that you get to live and learn.

Now let that sizzle in your spirit.

ACKNOWLEDGMENTS

When I first decided to write a book and to tell my story, complete with the most important lessons I've been fortunate to learn in my life, I was told by more than a few people—You? You're a comic not a serious author! For everyone who has ever told me, *No, you CAN'T,* at every stage of the game, I've been so blessed to have been guided to a handful of very special people who were always there to tell me, *Yes, you CAN.* That has never been more true than in my journey as a first-time author. And not only were there folks in my corner who believed in the story I wanted to write, but also, very fortunately, help was on the way to show me how to get it done.

The person I most want to thank is Mim Eichler Rivas for utilizing the gifts God gave her and capturing my story in a pure way. She let it speak to her and she viewed my journey with the same admiration and ambition that I have for my own. Mim treated the story we got to tell like it was hers and it became ours. I thank her for believing in it from day one and for staying persistent and patient throughout this journey.

I have to give a special shout-out to Matt Frost and the rest of my team at CAA, especially literary agent Anthony Mattero. Big thanks to you, Anthony, for seeing my vision, for encouraging me at every step of the writing, and guiding us to the perfect publishing home at Harmony/Penguin Random House. I could not have asked for a better editor than Matthew Benjamin—whose passion, patience, and precision are evident throughout the book. Thanks also to Diana Baroni, Anna Bauer, Serena Wang, Alison Hagge, Mia Pulido, and the rest of the in-house publishing team who have been pro all the way.

Sending props to Avi Gilbert and everyone at Fourth Wall management. Avi, I'm still working on the #mosesispoppin merchandise. There are so many people who help with my work on the road, with my production company, and who help mind the store while I'm gone. Without all of ya'll I wouldn't have found the time to write this book or do what I do. This is a collective thanks to everyone in the cast and crew of Kountry Wayne Entertainment who bring your talents to the set every day. Much love and gratitude to my family and, above all, to my kids—you are my reason for everything.

Last but not at all least, a heartfelt thanks to all the readers, audience members, fans, and strangers on the street for coming on this journey so far. Don't forget to drink lots of water and to know you are never alone because help is always on the way.

ABOUT THE AUTHOR

Dewayne "Kountry Wayne" Colley has earned a loyal following with his widely popular digital sketches and hilarious stand-up, generating an extraordinary amount of buzz as one of comedy's rising stars. With his humble roots and unbridled energy, Wayne continues to build his audience with cutting-edge, yet clean, material whose appeal transcends cultural lines.